The Place of the Bible in Education

An Appeal to Christians

By
Alonzo T. Jones

TEACH Services, Inc.
PUBLISHING
www.TEACHServices.com

World rights reserved. This book or any portion thereof may not be copied or reproduced in any form or manner whatever, except as provided by law, without the written permission of the publisher, except by a reviewer who may quote brief passages in a review.

This book was written to provide truthful information in regard to the subject matter covered. The author assumes full responsibility for the accuracy of all facts and quotations as cited in this book. The opinions expressed in this book are the author's personal views and interpretation of the Bible, Spirit of Prophecy, and/or contemporary authors and do not necessarily reflect those of TEACH Services, Inc.

This book is sold with the understanding that the publisher is not engaged in giving spiritual, legal, medical, or other professional advice. If authoritative advice is needed, the reader should seek the counsel of a competent professional

Copyright © 2005 TEACH Services, Inc.
ISBN-13: 978-57258-388-7
Library of Congress Control Number: 2005906232

Published by

www.TEACHServices.com

"To know wisdom and instruction: to perceive the words of understanding: to receive the instruction of wisdom, justice, judgment, and equity: to give subtilty to the simple, to the young man knowledge and discretion."—Prov. 1:2–4

CONTENTS

1. Christian Education 1
2. The World's Educations 5
3. The Essentials of Knowledge 13
4. The Secret of the Great Apostasy 23
5. The Greek or "Scientific Method" Today 31
6. The Separation of Christianity and the State 45
7. Bible's Right to Supreme Place in Christian Education . 55
8. The Education of Daniel 67
9. What Was Taught in the Schools of The Prophets 73
10. The Study of Wisdom 81
11. The Study of Knowledge 85
12. The Study of Science 89
13. The Study of Mental science 97
14. The Study of Moral Science 111
15. The Study of Physical Science 129
16. The Study of Physical Science—Anatomy 133
17. The Study of Physical Science—Healing 153
18. The Study of Physical Science—Physical Culture . . . 165
19. The Study of Physical Science—*Continued* 171
20. Literature, History, Law, Logic 181
21. The Failure of Popular Education 193

v

Chapter 1.

Christian Education.

WHATSOEVER is not Christian, is not becoming to Christians. A Christian education is the only education that can possibly be becoming to Christians. In Christian education the Book of Christianity must be preeminent. The Bible is the Book of Christianity.

The purpose of Christian education is to build up Christians. Nothing that is not Christian can ever properly be brought into the education of a Christian, any more than can anything that is not Christian be properly brought into any other phase of the life of the Christian. Therefore, the Book of Christianity,—the Bible,—must be the standard of Christian education; it must be the test of everything that enters into the education of a Christian; and it must supply all that is needed in the education of the Christian. And this contemplates education in the highest, broadest, and best sense—the all-round, practical development of the individual, mentally, physically, and morally.

It has been, and it is, too much supposed that Christianity has to do only with a sort of spiritualized existence, apart from the real occupations and practical things of life. This will never do. Christianity belongs in the deepest sense as a vital working force, in all that ever rightly can go to make up the sum of human life upon the earth. And Christian education is true to its name and profession only when it demonstrates this all-pervading power of Christianity as a vital element in all that can properly enter into the course of human life.

The Place of the Bible in Education

It can not be denied that the life of Christ is the demonstration of Christianity. He is the model Man: the Pattern of what every man must be to be a perfect Christian. And it is certain that Christ in human flesh demonstrating the Christian life on earth, put Himself in vital connection with every true relationship of human life upon this earth. He came into the world an infant; He grew up from infancy to manhood, as people in this world do; He met all that human beings in this world meet as they grow up; He met all the vicissitudes and experiences of human life, precisely, as to the fact, as all people meet them; for "in all things it behooved Him to be made like unto His brethren." He was "in all points tempted like as we are;" and He worked as a carpenter with Joseph, until the day of His showing unto Israel in the active work of His preaching, healing, ministry. And He was just as much the Saviour of the world when He was sawing boards and making benches and tables, as He was when He was preaching the sermon on the mount. And this demonstrates that Christianity just as truly and as vitally enters into the mechanical or other affairs of every-day life as it does into the preaching of the divinest sermon that was ever delivered.

And yet, in all this Jesus was only the Word made flesh. The Word of God, in written form, was in the world before Jesus came in the flesh; but through the blindness and hardness of heart of men, that Word was not allowed to manifest itself truly in the flesh. He came that this might be allowed. In Him, the Word that was here before He came, was made flesh, and dwelt among men, as the model Man. Since, then, Jesus was the Word made flesh, nothing appeared in His life on earth, that was not already in the Word. And since that which He was in the flesh was only what the Word was that was here before He came, it is certain that it was by the Word of God, through the Spirit of God, that He was made to be what He was, in the flesh. And this demonstrates that the Word of God, the Bible, the Book of Christianity, contains that which will completely educate mankind in an all-round, symmetrical life; and that no education is Christian that does not enter vitally into all the occupations and affairs of human life upon the earth.

The life of Christ, therefore, as it appeared upon the earth—that life being only the expression of the Word of God—causes to stand forth clearly and distinctly the great truth that the Bible, the Book of Christianity, is the greatest educational element, the greatest educational agency, the greatest educational Book, in the world. It is therefore true, that in the Word of God, the Bible, are "hid all the treasures of wisdom and knowledge," as truly as in Him, who in the flesh was but the expression of that Word. Accordingly, the Word of God is given, in order "that the man of God may be perfect, thoroughly furnished unto all good works."

This is the position which the Word of God occupied as an educational factor in the view of Christianity in ancient time, and this estimate is grandly echoed by that eminent Christian, the morning star of Christianity in modern times, John Wycliffe: "There is no subtlety, in grammar, neither in logic, nor in any other science that can be named, but that it is found in a more excellent degree in the Scriptures."

Chapter 2.

The World's Education.

WHEN Christianity, as such, began in the world, the Word of God was its educational Book. However, there was at that time in the world that which claimed to be education; and not only education, but *the only* education in any true sense. This which was claimed to be the true education, and which was accepted by the world as the only true education, had to be met by Christianity. And on this question of education, as in all other things, Christianity and the world were at direct opposites.

Christianity and this other education met at the then three great educational centers in the world; and we know how entirely at opposites they stood, because we have the words of Inspiration on the subject, defining exactly what that was which was held by the world to be education.

Corinth was one of the three educational centers in the world, at that time. "Corinth was the Vanity Fair of the Roman Empire; therefore, at once the London and the Paris of the first century after Christ."—*Farrar*. The great apostle to the Gentiles spent eighteen months in planting Christianity in that center of the world's education; and when he had gone away, he wrote concerning heathendom and its education, these words: "After that in the wisdom of God the world by wisdom knew not God, it pleased God by the foolishness of preaching to save them that believe." 1 Cor. 1:21.

The world had reached the point at which it did not know God. It was "by wisdom" that the world reached this

The Place of the Bible in Education

point. It was "by wisdom" that the world was caused not to know God. And that wisdom was the world's philosophy, the world's science,—in a word, the world's education. Therefore, Inspiration plainly shows that that which was accepted by the world as education, was itself the means of their not knowing God. But Christianity is the definite and certain knowledge of God. How could any two things be more directly at opposites, than are a system which causes men definitely and certainly to know, and a system which definitely causes men not to know?

Ephesus was another of the three educational centers of the world. It was the most magnificent of "the magnificent cities of Asia." "Its markets glittered with the produce of the world's arts—were the Vanity Fair of Asia. Nor was any name more splendidly emblazoned in the annals of human culture, than that of the great capital of Ionia."—*Farrar*. In that cultured and educational city the great apostle to the Gentiles conducted a Christian school nearly two and a half years: first in the synagogue "for the space of three months," and afterward, "when divers were hardened, and believed not, but spake evil of that way before the multitude, he departed from them, and separated the disciples, disputing daily in the school of one Tyrannus. And this continued by the space of two years." Acts 19:9, 10. He was establishing a distinctly Christian education as against a distinctly heathen education. That which led directly to the establishing of this specific *school* of Christian education, was that "divers were hardened, and believed not." Then, from the promiscuous audience, Paul separated the disciples, those who *believed*, and taught daily in the school of Tyrannus the way of Christian education. As a consequence many of the Gentiles of that cultured city became Christians. And when Paul wrote to the Ephesians, his epistle contained the following earnest words: "This I say therefore, and testify in the Lord, that ye henceforth walk not as other Gentiles walk, in the vanity

The World's Education.

of their mind, having the understanding darkened, being alienated from the life of God through the ignorance that is in them, because of the blindness of their heart." Eph. 4:17, 18.

These Gentile people of the city of Ephesus were alienated (separated, cut off) from the life of God through the ignorance that was in them. It was their ignorance that was the cause of their separation from the life of God. But Ephesus was a center of education; and it was precisely that education that caused their alienation from the life of God. Yet Inspiration declares that they were alienated from the life of God through the *ignorance* that was in them. It is, therefore, perfectly plain, that Inspiration defines their education to have been ignorance.

Athens was the third of these great centers of the world's education. Athens was more than this: she was *the mother* of the then world's education. Yea, she was even more than this: she was the mother, in a large sense, of that which has been the world's education to this day. And to Athens also went the great apostle to the Gentiles. There he was brought before the Supreme Court, to be heard as to what bearing his teachings were having in the matter of being a "setter forth of strange gods." And twice in his speech before that Court, and the assembled crowd, Inspiration uses the precise word that was used with reference to the world's education in Ephesus. He said: "Ye men of Athens, I perceive that in all things ye are too superstitious. For as I passed by, and beheld your devotions, I found an altar with this inscription, TO THE UNKNOWN GOD. Whom therefore ye *ignorantly* worship, Him declare I unto you. God that made the world and all things therein, seeing that He is Lord of heaven and earth, dwelleth not in temples made with hands; neither is worshiped with men's hands, as though He needed anything, seeing He giveth to all life, and breath, and all things; and hath made of one blood all nations of men for to dwell on all the face of the

The Place of the Bible in Education

earth, and hath determined the times before appointed, and the bounds of their habitation; that they should seek the Lord, if haply they might feel after Him, and find Him, though He be not far from every one of us; for in Him we live, and move, and have our being; as certain also of your own poets have said, For we are also His offspring.

"Forasmuch then as we are the offspring of God, we ought not to think that the Godhead is like unto gold, or silver, or stone, graven by art and man's device. And the times of this *ignorance* God winked at; but now commandeth all men everywhere to repent; because He hath appointed a day, in the which He will judge the world in righteousness by that Man whom He hath ordained; whereof He hath given assurance unto all men, in that He hath raised Him from the dead." Acts 17:22–31.

They had erected an altar in honor of the unknown God. In this, they "ignorantly worshiped." That city was wholly given to idolatry, for it was full of idols of gold, or silver, or stone, graven by art and man's device, expressing their ideas of God; and "the times of this *ignorance*" God endured, but now commanded "all men everywhere to repent" of this "ignorance." But do not forget that all this was but a part, the central part indeed, of the education of Athens, of the education which she imparted, of the education of which she was the mother. For that education culminated in art; that art was idolatry; and that idolatry was but the manifestation of ignorance. Therefore, again it is demonstrated that the world's education, Greek education, at that time, was only ignorance. And when it is understood how supremely Athens prided herself upon the education which she gave to the world, some faint estimate can be formed of the depth of the spirit of their mockery in response to the word of a despised Jew, standing in such a presence, and defining it all as "ignorance," and calling upon them to repent of their education.

The World's Education.

Yet ignorance is precisely, and only, what it was. That alter with its inscription "TO THE UNKNOWN GOD," was but a monument erected to their ignorance. For that word "ignorance" which Inspiration uses, is not merely a term captiously used, to imply that the world's education was *equivalent* to ignorance, and was *ultimately* ignorance in that it did not attain to the knowledge of God; but it is a word definitely selected by Inspiration as truly defining, in its very essence, the real character of that education: that it was in itself "ignorance." This is clearly seen when it is understood what the principle and the process of that education were. This is given by accepted authority.

Socrates was the great educator of Greece; and Greece, through Plato and Aristotle, was the educator of the world. And of Socrates it is written:—

> "Socrates was not a 'philosopher,' nor yet a 'teacher,' but rather an 'educator,' having for his function to rouse, persuade, and rebuke.'—*Plato, Apology, 30 E*. Hence, in examining his life's work, it is proper to ask, not, 'What was his philosophy?' but, 'What was his theory, and what was his practice, of *education?* He was brought to his theory of education by the study of previous philosophies, and his practice led to the Platonic revival.
>
> "*Socrates' theory of education has for its basis a* PROFOUND AND CONSISTENT SKEPTICISM.
>
> "Taking his departure from some apparently remote principle or proposition to which the respondent yielded a ready assent, Socrates would draw from it an unexpected but undeniable consequence which was plainly inconsistent with the opinion impugned. In this way, he brought his interlocutor to pass judgment upon himself, and reduced him to a state of 'doubt,' or 'perplexity.' 'Before I ever met you,' says Meno in the Dialogue which Plato called by his name, 'I was told that you spent your time in doubting, and leading others to doubt; and it is a fact that your

The Place of the Bible in Education

witcheries and spells have brought me to that condition.'"—*Encyclopedia Britannica*, article "Socrates."

Plato was the pupil and reporter of Socrates. Socrates himself left no writings. It is to Plato that the world owes almost all that it knows of Socrates, especially as to his "philosophy." Thus, in the field of philosophy, speculation, metaphysics, Plato is the great voice and continuator of Socrates. Aristotle was a disciple of Plato; but he broke away from the particularly philosophical and metaphysical speculations of his master, and turned specially to science and physics. Plato leaned to having all things culminate in philosophy. Aristotle leaned toward having all things culminate in science: he would "reduce even philosophy to science." And Aristotle like Plato continued in education the identical principle of education which was entertained by Socrates and continued by Plato: that doubt is the way to knowledge. For with Aristotle it was a maxim that "to frame doubts well" is a service to the discovery of truth.

Thus, then, as stated concerning Socrates, the basis of the whole theory of Greek education, both in science and philosophy, was "*doubt*,"—"a profound and consistent skepticism." Indeed, the principal idea of that philosophy is expressed in the word "doubt." The history of philosophy is but the history of doubt.

Now, the essential characteristic and quality of doubt is that it definitely causes him who exercises it, not to know. So long as any one doubts a thing, he can not know that thing. And not to know, is simply ignorance. Since, therefore, the basis of the great Greek educator's theory of education was "doubt,"—"a profound and consistent skepticism;" and since the essential quality of doubt causes him who exercises it not to know; it follows that Greek education, being founded in doubt, and built up through doubt, was essentially ignorance. And Inspiration pierced to the very core of the whole system when it repeatedly

The World's Education.

defined that education as "ignorance." And the word "ignorance" was definitely chosen by the Spirit of Inspiration simply because it essentially defined the thing.

Chapter 3.

The Essentials to Knowledge.

WE may be told that which is veritably true, the essential truth of God; yet if we doubt it, and so long as we doubt it, we never can know it. Therefore, doubt is essentially and only the open door to ignorance.

Further, we may be told that which is altogether false, an outright lie; yet though we believe it, however implicitly, we never can know it. This, for the simple reason that it is not so; and it is impossible to know what is not so.

Therefore there are just two things which are essential to knowing. These two things are *truth* and *faith*.

Truth and faith are the two essentials to knowledge: and the first of these in order is *truth*. This, for the reason already stated, that however implicitly we may believe that which is not so, we never can know it. Therefore, since that which is believed must be *true* in order to be known, it follows that truth is the first essential to knowledge. And since even the sincerest truth, when told, can not be known without our believing it, it follows that the second essential to knowledge is *faith*. Truth and faith, therefore, working together—the truth believed—is the way to knowledge.

This can be illustrated by an experience familiar to almost all. It is the truth that A is A. We *believed* this *truth*, and thus, and thus only, we *know* that A is A. If we had not believed that truth when we were told it, we should not now know that A, B, C, D, etc., are what they are; and had we never believed this, we never could have known it. If in

The Place of the Bible in Education

this we had asked for *proof* as a basis for belief, we never could have had it, and so never could have believed, and so never could have known this fundamental thing in all literary knowledge. We could have had no proof, apart from itself, that A or any other letter of the alphabet is what it is.

There is proof of this, but the proof is in the letter itself; and by believing it, by receiving it for what it is we obtain the knowledge; and in this knowledge and by experience we obtain the proof. For in each of the letters of the alphabet there is a value which responded to our belief: a value which has never failed and which never will fail us. We *know* that each of the letters is what it is: and all the philologists, philosophers, and scientists in all the world could not convince us that any letter of the alphabet is other than it simply is. And yet the *means* by which we know this is simple *belief* of a simple, and simply-told, *truth*.

This thought, this illustration, does not stop here. The first two letters of the Greek alphabet are *Alpha* and *Beta*. Dropping the "a" from Beta, these two Greek letters give us our word *Alpha-bet*. This word "alphabet" signifies all the letters of the English language. How comes this, when the word itself is derived from only the first *two* of the letters of the Greek language? It comes in a very simple way. When we in our language wish to ask whether a person knows, or we wish to say that a person does not know, the alphabet, we most commonly ask *not*. "Does he know the alphabet?" nor, "Does he know the A B C D E F G H I J K L M N." and so on through to "Z?" but we ask, "Does he know the A B C's?" or we say, "He does not know his A B C's." The Greeks did the same way: When they wished to express the same thought, they did not say, "Does he know the Alpha, Beta, Gamma, Delta, Epsilon," and so on to "Omega?" but simply, "Does he know the Alpha Beta?" or, "He does not know the Alpha Beta." And this Greek abbreviation of the whole list of the letters of that language into only "Alpha Beta" comes down to us

The Essentials to Knowledge.

with the dropping of the "a" from Beta; and so becomes our word "alphabet," the abbreviation of the whole list of the letters of our language.

In common English there is a concise way of saying that a person knows little or nothing of a subject, in the expression, "He does not know the A B C of it." The Greeks had the same, "He does not know the Alpha Beta of it." On the other hand, there is a concise way of saying that a person is thoroughly informed, or knows all of a subject, in the expression, "He knows that subject from A to Z," or, old style, "from A to Izzard" The Greeks had the same, "He knows that subject from Alpha to Omega"—he knows all there is to be known of it. *And this is the basis and the thought* in the expression of Christ in the book of Revelation several times, "*I am Alpha and Omega*, the beginning and the end, the first and the last."

Jesus is the Alphabet of God. As the expression "Alpha and Omega" signifies the whole alphabet, and embraces all there is in the Greek language; and "A to Z" signifies the whole alphabet, all that there is in the English language; so Jesus Christ, the Alphabet of God, embraces all that there is of the language or knowledge of God. As in the twenty-four letters of the Greek Alphabet from Alpha to Omega there are hid all the treasures of wisdom and knowledge in the world of that language; and as in the twenty-six letters of the English alphabet there are hid all the treasures of wisdom and knowledge that there are in the world of the English language; so in Jesus Christ, the Alphabet of God, there are "hid all the treasures of wisdom and knowledge" that there are in the universe of the language of God.

And this Alphabet of God is learned in precisely the same way and with precisely the same faculty as is the alphabet of Greek, or English, or any other language. The Alphabet of God is the truth. We *believe* that *truth* and thus we *know* that He is what He is. There is proof of this, but the proof is in Himself. By *believing* this Alphabet, by receiving Him for what He is, we obtain the *knowledge*; and in this knowledge and by experience of it we have the constant living proof. For in this Alphabet of God, in each letter, yea, in each jot and tittle, there is a value that responds to our faith: a value that never has failed, that never will fail, and that never can fail, to respond to any man's belief of that Alphabet. And to him who thus *knows* the Alphabet of God, all the philosophers and all the scientists and all the unbelievers in all the world can not prove to him that any part of this Alphabet is not what He is. Indeed, any one attempting to prove any such thing only thereby reveals the fact that he does not yet know the true Alphabet: he does not yet know his A B C's.

It is only as a little child that we learn, it is only as a little child any one can learn, the alphabet of the English language. Though a man were a thousand years old, and fully possessed of all his faculties, and yet did not know the A B C's, the alphabet of English, he would have to become as a little child in order to learn it, in order to receive the knowledge that A is A: he would have to simply believe it as does the little child, and by *believing* that each letter is what it is, when he were told, he would *know*. And if he should refuse to believe this, by this very refusal—by his unbelief itself—he would be condemned—he would thus condemn himself—to everlasting loss of all the treasures of wisdom and knowledge that are hid in the world of English.

So also it is with the Alphabet of the language and knowledge of God. It is only by believing *this* Alphabet that any person can ever *know* Him. If any one refuses to believe, he can not know. And whosoever believeth not is by this very unbelief condemned—he by this condemns himself—to everlasting loss of all the treasures of wisdom and knowledge of God: all of which lie hidden in the Alphabet of God. For as it is by various combinations of the

The Essentials to Knowledge.

contents of the alphabet that words are formed, and words express thought; so the manifold combinations of the contents of the Alphabet of God form the Word of God, and the Word of God expresses the thought of God.

Therefore Jesus Christ announced the eternal principle of true learning when He declared, "Whosoever shall not receive the kingdom of God as a little child shall in nowise enter therein." The little child does receive the kingdom of God. He receives it by simply believing the simple statement of the Word of the kingdom. This is how every one receives, and how every one must receive, the kingdom of English or of any other language. It is how every one must receive the kingdom of God. To receive the kingdom of God, and to know the Alphabet of God, is as easy as to know the A B C's. Therefore to learn, *not* as a *philosopher*, but as a *little child*, is the true way to knowledge. The truth and faith, working together—the truth believed—is forever the true way to knowledge.

Accordingly when God would seek to save the world from the ruin of its ignorance, He did it by presenting to the world the *truth to be believed*. "For after that in the wisdom of God the world by wisdom knew not God, it pleased God by the foolishness of preaching [the preaching of the Word, which is the truth: the preaching of Christ, who is the Truth] to save them *that believe*. For the Jews require a sign, and the Greeks seek after wisdom; but we preach Christ crucified, unto the Jews a stumbling-block, and unto the Greeks foolishness; but unto them which are called, both Jews and Greeks, Christ the power of God, and the wisdom of God." 1 Cor. 1:21–24.

We have read the words of Inspiration that it was by wisdom that the world knew not (was ignorant of) God. We have also read the words of Inspiration that the Gentiles were alienated (separated, cut off) from the life of God,

The Place of the Bible in Education

through the ignorance that was in them. We have seen that in the wisdom of God, and in the essential truth of the case, the world's wisdom was ignorance: and that not only was the world in its ignorance alienated from the life of God, but that it was *by this ignorance itself* that the world was alienated from the life of God.

Since, then, it is the characteristic of ignorance to separate men from the life of God; on the other hand, it is the characteristic of knowledge that it joins men to the life of God, which is eternal life. Accordingly, it is written. "This is life eternal, that they might know Thee the only true God, and Jesus Christ, whom Thou hast sent." This is equally true, read only in the words, "This is life eternal, that they *might know.*" So that, as certainly as ignorance, being the product of doubt, by which men can not know, alienates men from the life of God; so certainly knowledge, being the product of faith in the truth, by which men certainly know, unites men to the life of God.

We have seen that it is belief of the truth alone which brings men to knowledge: and since Jesus Christ is "the Truth," it follows that faith in Christ as the Word of God is the only way to knowledge. Accordingly, again, Inspiration draws clearly the distinction between the world of Greek wisdom, which was ignorance; and faith in Christ, which is the way of knowledge. And so it is written[1]: "My aim is that they may be encouraged, and be bound to one another by love, so attaining to the full blessedness of a firm and intelligent conviction, and to a perfect knowledge of God's secret truths which are *embodied in Christ.* For *all God's treasures of wisdom and knowledge are to be found* STORED UP IN CHRIST. I say this to prevent any one deceiving you by plausible arguments. It is true that I am not with you in person, but I am with you in spirit: and I

---

1 The *Twentieth Century New Testament* translation of this passage (Col. 2:2–10) is so expressive that it is here used.

The Essentials to Knowledge.

rejoice to know of your good order and of the solid front which you present through your faith in Christ.

"Since, then, you have received Jesus, the Christ, as your Lord, live your lives in union with Him—rooted in Him, building up your lives upon Him, growing stronger through your faith, *true to the teaching you received*, rich in faith, and always giving thanks. Take care there is not some one who will capture you by his 'philosophy'—a hollow sham! Such teaching follows mere human traditions, and has to do with puerile questions of the world, and not with Christ. For *the Godhead in all its fulness dwells in Christ in a bodily form*; and, by your union with Him, you also are filled with it."

Again, this contrast between the world's ignorance and God's knowledge is clearly drawn in 1 Cor. 1:18 to 2:10, and, as translated in the Twentieth Century version, reads: "The Message of the Cross is indeed mere folly to people who are on the way to Ruin, but to us who are on the way to Salvation it is the very power of God. Indeed, Scripture says—

"'I will bring the wisdom of the wise to nothing,

"'And make the cleverness of the clever of no account.'

"Where are the wise men? or the teachers of religion? or the critical people of today? Has not God shown the world's wisdom to be folly? For since the world, in God's wisdom, did not by its own wisdom get to know God, God saw fit, by the 'folly' of our proclamation, to save those who believe it! While Jews are asking for miraculous signs and Greeks are seeking for wisdom, we are proclaiming Christ who has been crucified! To the Jews He is an obstacle, to the heathen He is mere folly, but to those who have received the Call, whether Jews or Greeks, He is Christ—God's power and God's wisdom. For God's 'folly' is wiser than men, and God's 'weakness' is stronger than men!

The Place of the Bible in Education

"Look, Brothers, at the facts of your Call. There are not many among you who are wise as men reckon wisdom, not many who are influential, not many who are high-born; but God chose what the world calls foolish to put its wise men to shame, and God chose what the world calls weak to put its 'strength' to shame, and God chose those whom the world calls low-born and beneath regard—mere nobodies—to put down its 'somebodies,' so that in His presence no human being should boast. But you, by your union with Christ Jesus, are God's offspring; and Christ, by God's will, became not only our Wisdom, but also our Righteousness, our Holiness, our Deliverance, so that—in the words of Scripture—'Let those who boast, boast about the Lord!'

"For my own part, Brothers, when I came to you, I did not come to tell you of the secret truths of God in the fine language of philosophy; for I had determined that, while with you, I would know nothing but Jesus Christ—and Him as one crucified! Indeed, when I found myself among you, I felt weak and timid and greatly agitated. My Message and my Proclamation were not delivered in the persuasive language of philosophy; but they were accompanied by manifestations of spiritual power, so that your faith should be based, not on the wisdom of man, but on the power of God.

"Yet what we speak of among those whose faith is matured is really wisdom, but it is not the wisdom of today nor the wisdom of the leaders of today—men whose downfall is at hand. No, the wisdom we speak of, when we deal with secret truths, is divine; it is the long-hidden wisdom, which God, before time began, decreed, that it might bring us glory. This wisdom is not known to any of the leaders of today.

Had they known it, they would not have crucified our glorious Master. But Scripture speaks of it as

"'What no eye ever saw, what no ear ever heard,

The Essentials to Knowledge.

"'What never entered the mind of man—

"'All that God prepared for those who love Him.'

"Yet to us God revealed it through His Spirit; for the Spirit fathoms everything, even the profoundest secrets of God."

Chapter 4.

The Secret of the Great Apostasy.

IN spite of the infinite contrast repeatedly drawn by Inspiration in the Scriptures between Greek ignorance and Christian knowledge, Christianity had barely become rooted in the world before there were those amongst the Christians who began to incline to the world's way, and to claim virtue for Greek ignorance. And this was the origin of the great apostasy.

The exaltation of worldly wisdom, which was but Greek ignorance, was the secret of the "falling away" from the truth of the gospel. And the divine warning against this thing was especially urged to the Ephesians. First, in the letter to the Ephesians, as follows: "This, then, is what I say unto you and urge upon you in the Lord's name. Do not continue to live as the heathen are living in their perverseness. Owing to the ignorance existing among them and the hardening of their hearts, their powers of discernment are darkened, and they are cut off from the Life of God. For lost to all sense of shame, they have abandoned themselves to licentiousness, in order to practice every kind of impurity without restraint.

"But as for you, FAR DIFFERENT *is the lesson that you learnt from the Christ*—if, that is, you really listened to Him, and by living in union with Him were taught *the Truth*, as it is *to be found in Jesus*. For you learnt with regard to your former life that you must lay aside your old nature, which, owing to the passions fostered by Error, was in a corrupt state; and that you must undergo a mental and spiritual transformation, and once for all clothe yourselves with a new nature—one made to resemble God in the righteousness and holiness demanded by *the Truth.*" Eph. 4:17–24.

And again, at that important meeting when, from Miletus, Paul "sent to Ephesus, and called the elders of the church," in his address to them, he spoke thus: "Take heed therefore unto yourselves, and to all the flock, over the which the Holy Ghost hath made you overseers, to feed the church of God, which He hath purchased with His own blood. For I know this, that after my departing shall grievous wolves enter in among you, not sparing the flock. Also of your own selves shall men arise, speaking perverse things, to draw away disciples after them. Therefore watch, and remember, that by the space of three years I ceased not *to warn every one night and day* with tears. And now, brethren, I commend you to God, *and to the word of His grace,* which is able to build you up, and to give you an inheritance among all them which are sanctified." Acts 20:28–32.

This apostasy was the burden of the apostle's warning, not only at Ephesus, but in other places. At Thessalonica, both in his preaching and in his letter to the Thessalonians, he dwelt much upon this. For concerning the day of the coming of the Lord in glory, having in his first letter written much of this, he wrote to them in his second letter thus: "As to the coming of Jesus Christ, our Lord, and our being gathered to meet Him, we beg you, Brothers, not lightly to let your minds become unsettled, nor yet to be alarmed by any so-called 'inspired' statement, or by any message, or by any letter, purporting to come from us, to the effect that the day of the Master is here. Do not let any one deceive you, try as they may. For come it will not, until after the Great Apostasy and the appearing of that Incarnation of Wickedness, who is born for destruction, and who opposes himself to every one that is spoken of as a God or as an object of worship, and so exalts himself

The Secret of the Great Apostasy.

above them that he seats himself in the Temple of God, and displays himself as actually being God!" 2 Thess. 2:1–4. Then, after having thus stated what that apostasy would reveal, he appeals to the memory of the Thessalonians, thus: "Do you not recollect how, when I was with you, I used to speak to you of all this?"

Much more is said of this in the Scriptures, but there is no need to cite more of it here. This is sufficient to enable all to see how certainly the apostasy was connected with the bringing in of worldly ignorance, and the mingling of it with the knowledge of God. And it was only in proportion that worldly ignorance—science falsely so called—was brought in, that the apostasy grew. And when the apostasy gained the ascendancy, it was but the ascendancy, under the Christian name, of the original Pagan Greek philosophy and science—Greek ignorance—in the professed Christian Church.

Against this evil, the apostles preached, wrote, and warned, all their days. For they saw the enormous consequences that must result from the entertainment only of the small beginnings that were apparent, even in their day. Yet in less than fifty years after the death of the last of the apostles, this apostasy had become so prominent that there were schools of it conducted under the Christian name and passing for Christian schools. The leaders in this thing, the heads of these schools, made the so-called philosophy of the world their standard; and amongst the standard world's philosophers they regarded Plato as "wiser than all the rest, and as especially remarkable for treating the Deity, the soul, and things remote from sense, so as to suit the Christian scheme."—*Mosheim*.

This thing was readily adopted by large classes of would-be philosophers and their imitators, who thus could assume the credit of being Christians without any of the self-denial or the correction of the inner life that is

The Place of the Bible in Education

essential to Christian experience. The same old heathen life could be maintained under the name and profession of Christianity. This evil made such progress that it was not long before

> "the estimation in which human learning should be held was a question upon which the Christians were *about equally divided*. Many recommended the study of philosophy and an acquaintance with the Greek and Roman literature; while others maintained that these were pernicious to the interests of genuine Christianity and the progress of true piety.
>
> "The cause of letters and philosophy triumphed, however, by degrees; and those who wished well to them continued to gain ground, till at length the superiority was manifestly decided in their favor. This victory was principally due to the influence of Origen, who, having been early instructed in the new kind of Platonism already mentioned, blended it, though unhappily, with the purer and more sublime tenets of a celestial doctrine, and recommended it in the warmest manner to the youth who attended his public lessons. The fame of this philosopher increased daily among the Christians; and in proportion to his rising credit, his method of proposing and explaining the doctrines of Christianity gained authority, till it became almost universal."—Ibid.

The position of Origen at that time may be estimated from the fact that to this day he is one of the chiefest of the Fathers of the church; and from the further fact that "from the days of Origen to those of Chrysostom [A. D. 220–400], there was not a single eminent commentator who did not borrow largely from the works of" Origen; and "he was the chief teacher of even the most orthodox of the Western Fathers." "Innumerable expositors in this and the following centuries pursued the method of Origen, though with

The Secret of the Great Apostasy.

some diversity; nor could the few who pursued a better method make much head against them."

But
> "this new species of philosophy, imprudently adopted by Origen and other Christians, did immense harm to Christianity. For it led the teachers of it to involve in philosophic obscurity many parts of our religion, which were in themselves plain, and easy to be understood; and to add to the precepts of the Saviour no few things of which not a word can be found in the Holy Scriptures....It recommended to Christians various foolish and useless rites, suited only to nourish superstition, no small part of which we see religiously observed by many even to the present day. And finally, it alienated the minds of many in the following centuries from Christianity itself; and produced a heterogeneous species of religion, consisting of Christian and Platonic principles combined. And who is able to enumerate all the evils and injurious changes that arose from this new philosophy—or, if you please, *from this attempt to reconcile* TRUE AND FALSE RELIGIONS with each other?"—*Mosheim.*

The result of all this is expressed in the one word—"the Papacy," as it has been, and as it is. Then occurred a curious though perfectly logical thing: In order to be "scientific," the apostasy adopted that pagan science falsely so called. Then, when she had filled the world with this pagan ignorance *as Christian knowledge*, and true science in the simple reading of nature sought recognition, she anathematized, and prohibited, and persecuted it.

That philosophic trend, as already stated, found its spring in Plato. But when it is borne in mind that Plato was only the reporter and continuator of Socrates, who was the great Greek educator, the basis of whose system of education was only "a profound and consistent skepticism," it is plainly seen that this system of the new Platonism which made the Papacy was nothing else than the system of

The Place of the Bible in Education

Greek education swung in under the Christian name, and passed off as Christian knowledge when it was only Pagan ignorance.

And *this* is "how" it is that "we are to account for the supreme elevation of this man [Plato] in the intellectual history of our race." *This* is "how it happens that the writings of Plato have preoccupied every school of learning, every lover of thought, every church, every poet,—making it impossible to think, on certain levels, except through him." This is how it is that "he stands between the truth and every man's mind, and has almost impressed language, and the primary forms of thought, with his name and seal."—*Representative Men*, by Ralph Waldo Emerson, page 46. And this is also how it is, that "in the history of European thought and knowledge, down to the period of the revival of letters, the name of Aristotle was without a rival, supreme....It even came to pass that, for a long period, all secular writings but those of Aristotle had dropped out of use in Europe....All sought in Aristotle the basis of knowledge. Universities and grammar schools were founded in Aristotle."—*Encyclopedia Britannica*, article "Aristotle."

And *this*, in turn, is how it is that when Christianity was revived for modern times, in the great Reformation, when Luther began to preach Christianity, and to introduce Christian education anew into the world, he was compelled to meet, to renounce, and to denounce, Aristotle, and other teachers of "a deceitful-philosophy," as follows: —

"Do not attach yourself to Aristotle, or to other teachers of a deceitful philosophy; but diligently read the Word of God."

"He who says that a theologian who is not a logician is an heretic and an adventurer, maintains an adventurous and heretical proposition.

The Secret of the Great Apostasy.

"There is no form of syllogism which accords with the things of God.[2]

"In one word, Aristotle is to theology as darkness to light."

"Aristotle, that blind heathen, has displaced Christ."

And again, of education wholly: "I much fear the universities will become wide gates to hell, if due care is not taken to explain the Holy Scriptures and engrave it on the hearts of the students. My advice to every person is, not to place his child where the Scripture does not reign paramount. Every institution in which the studies carried on lead to a relaxed consideration of the Word of God must prove corrupting."

And it was the double placing of the worldly ignorance of Greek philosophy and logic—Plato and Aristotle—above the divine knowledge of the Word of God, that, at the very beginning of this revival of Christianity for modern times, led Wycliffe to declare that "there is no subtlety in grammar, neither in logic, nor in any other science that can be named, but that it is found in a more excellent degree in the Scriptures."

Such was the key-note of the Reformation. And though to the sincere Christian it is all so plain and true; yet after the death of Luther, when the apostasy of Protestantism had begun to come in, in less than one hundred years Aristotle was again given the chief place in the seats of learning, and the Greek system of education was continued; so that today it reigns supreme in the schools of both the Church and the State, even in professed Christian and Protestant lands.

---

2   The special point in this will be more clearly seen when it is understood that in the Greek system, *logic* was the test of *truth*: than which it would be impossible to make a greater mistake.

Chapter 5.

The Greek or "Scientific Method" Today.

IT is certain that Christianity, in ancient times, and at its revival in modern times, found, and held, and proclaimed, that the Bible, the Holy Scriptures, the Word of God, is the only true and sufficient basis of an all-round education for Christians. Disregard of this principle in the early days of Christianity developed the Papacy; and disregard of this principle in these last days of Christianity is developing through Protestantism a repetition of the course of the Papacy.

To professed Protestantism today, the Bible is not held in any true sense as an educational book. The science of the unbelieving world, the philosophy and the literature of ancient Greece and Rome, have a far larger place than has the Bible, in that which is recognized by Protestants as education. The highest course in college or university is the classical; and this course derives its title of "classical" from the fact that the literature of Greece and Rome is the predominant element in the course. This is true, even with those who are studying for the ministry of the gospel of Christ. But how the study, for years, of literature which is essentially Pagan can be a preparation for the preaching of the gospel which must be wholly Christian, no one has attempted to explain.

Not only is worldly science and Pagan literature more courted by Protestantism than is the Bible, in education; but the very theory of education held by Socrates, and continued by Plato and Aristotle,—"doubt," "a profound and consistent skepticism,"—is held today in the education recognized by Protestantism, in school, college, university, and even in the theological seminary. For instance, the *Outlook* of April 21, 1900, in describing and urging "A Needed Educational Reform," says: —

> "The educational processes of our time,—possibly of all time,—are largely analytical and critical. They consist chiefly in analyzing the subjects brought to the student for his examination, separating them into their constituent parts, considering how they have been put together, and sitting in judgment on the finished fabric. or on the process by which it has been constructed....The process presupposes an inquiring, if not a skeptical, mood. *Doubt is the pedagogue which leads the pupil to knowledge.*"

And in the *North American Review* for April, 1900, there was published an article entitled "The Scientific Method in Theology," written by a professor of philosophy in Union College, Schenectady, N. Y.; who was educated at Amherst and Yale; spent two years in philosophical study in Germany; and from 1883 to 1885 was instructor of philosophy in Wesleyan University. Thus, every circumstance of the article is a pledge that it is authoritative as to the scientific method in theology, and in that article it is said: —

> "Every man, because he is a man, is endowed with powers for forming judgments, and he is placed in this world to develop and apply those powers to all objects with which he comes in contact. In *every sphere of investigation*, he should *begin with* DOUBT, and the student will make *the most rapid progress* who has acquired the *art of doubting well.*...We ask that every student of theology take up the subject precisely as he would any other science: that he *begin with* DOUBT."

The Greek or "Scientific Method" Today.

It never can be denied that this is simply the repetition in modern times of the Socratic theory of education. And this, not only in college and university, but in the theological seminary where young men are professedly to be trained in "the science concerned with ascertaining, classifying, and systematizing all attainable truth concerning God, and His relation to the universe; the science of religion; religious truth scientifically studied." This, not only in college and university, where men are to be fitted only for the everyday affairs of the world; but in a professedly Christian school, where men are to be fitted preeminently for the Christian profession, and to be educators in Christianity.

In every sphere of investigation, the student is taught and expected to "begin with doubt," in this study of the science of the "truth concerning God." And this when the truth of God itself, given in His own Word, is that "without *faith* it is impossible to please Him;" and "whatsoever is not of *faith* is sin." Since, then, God has stated it, that "without *faith* it is impossible to please Him," and "whatsoever is not of *faith* is sin;" and since, in the theological seminaries of professed Christianity, the student is expected, "in every sphere of investigation," to "begin with doubt," it is certain that in that system of education, every student is systematically taught to begin in the way in which it is impossible to please God, and which is only the way of sinning. And this as the preparation for the ministry of the gospel!

This authoritative statement of the scientific method in theology shows that even in the Protestant schools of today, in which is taught particularly the science of the knowledge of God, the process is directly opposite to that which is stated in the Word of the Lord Himself. God has said that "he that cometh to God *must believe* that He is, and [*must believe*] that He is a rewarder of them that diligently seek Him." The "scientific method" of education today, even in Protestant schools which teach the science of God, is inevitably that he who cometh to God must *doubt* that He is, and *must doubt* that He is a rewarder of them that diligently seek Him.

The result of such a process can not possibly be anything else than that a man—each individual for himself, or else, and ultimately, a representative for all—shall put himself above God; and there, sitting as judge, subject the wisdom and knowledge of God to the dictates of human reason.

Nor is this simply a deduction from the quotation already made, though it is clearly deducible from that quotation. It is actually stated in this article in the sentences immediately following the one already quoted:—

> "We ask that every student of theology take up the subject precisely as he would any other science: that he *begin with doubt*, and carefully weigh the arguments for every doctrine, *accepting or rejecting each assertion*, according as the balance of probabilities is for or against it. We demand that he thoroughly 'test all things,' and thus learn how to 'hold fast that which is good.' We believe that *even the teachings of Jesus should be viewed from this standpoint*, and should be *accepted* or *rejected* on the ground of their *inherent reasonableness*."

Thus, reason being set above Jesus Christ—who is God manifest—to analyze, to criticize, to judge, His teachings, for acceptance or rejection, *as the individual's doubting reason shall decide*—this is manifestly to set reason above God: which, in turn, is to put reason itself in the place of God as God.

Follow this process a little in its direct working, and see how completely it lands today precisely where Inspiration declares that it landed in its original course, and in its prime:—

The Greek or "Scientific Method" Today.

"The great and distinctive element in all induction is *the formation of the hypothesis*, and there can be no inductive science formed, of any sort, where this is not the chief feature.

"What, then, is to be understood by an hypothesis? And what is the process the mind goes through in bringing it to view?—An hypothesis is *a supposition*, a *guess*, or *conjecture*, as to what the general effect is which includes the given particular effects, or what the cause is which has brought about the given effects.

"Much might be said about the conditions most favorable for the making of a good hypothesis; but the chief thing that concerns us for our present purpose is the fact that every hypothesis, however formed, is always the product of the *constructive imagination*. All previous acts are simply by way of gathering material for *the imagination* to rearrange, and recombine into a *new creation*....

"It is for this reason that men of science, in all realms and in all ages, have always been men of powerful imaginations. *The Greeks* were *the first great scientists of the race*, because they were far more highly endowed than any other people with *great imaginative powers*. What they saw, excited these powers, and urged them to conjecture, to reason about things, and try to explain their nature and cause."

There is here no room to inquire whether or not this process today lands where landed the same process in ancient Greece; because that is where precisely, in so many words, the article itself lands. And how could this process be more fittingly described than it is in the Scripture, written directly as descriptive of this identical process in ancient time: "When they knew God, they glorified Him not as God, neither were thankful; but became vain in *their imaginations*, and their foolish heart was darkened. Professing themselves to be wise, they became fools, and changed the glory of the uncorruptible God into an image made like to corruptible man, and to birds, and four-footed beasts, and creeping things." Rom. 1:21–23.

And how can the rest of the description there given (Rom. 1:24–32) be escaped, when this process shall be followed today? For even in the quotation last above made, it is admitted that the scientific method in theology today is identical with that of old, of which the Greeks, "the first great scientists of the race," were the exemplars; and this, "because they were far more highly endowed than any other people with great *imaginative powers*." And their exercise of these "great imaginative powers" in precisely the way above outlined, did lead them into the condition which is described in the remaining verses of the first chapter of Romans.

And yet, this process, by means of "the constructive imagination," contemplates "a new creation"! And who shall be the creator in this new creation?—None other than the human individual himself, who by guesses gathers "material for the imagination to rearrange, and recombine, into a new creation." This, then, makes man a creator in the place of the Creator.

Follow yet further the scientific process in theology, and see what is the ground upon which its followers land, as to knowledge: —

> "Given the hypothesis, the next step in the scientific process is to verify it: and this is done by making the hypothesis the major premise of a deductive syllogism, and noting the results. If the conclusions coincide with the obtained facts, with which we started, the hypothesis is *probably* the correct one [the italics here are the author's]; and other things being equal, may be accepted as established truth. From this outline of the scientific method, we see that no induction can be established beyond a high degree of probability; that is, no one can ever be absolutely certain that the hypothesis he assumes is veritably true. All

The Greek or "Scientific Method" Today.

> generalizations in every science thus have their logical basis in the theory of probabilities.
>
> "When Bishop Butler asserted that 'probability is the very guide of life,' he might have added, 'and we have no other.'...
>
> "Great thinkers, from Thales, Plato, and Moses, have had their theologies,—their explanations of the origin of the universe, as they understood it,—and many of these explanations have been of extraordinary merit; but even St. Paul himself could never have been certain that his explanation was more than a probably true one."

Than is therein stated, how could it be possible more clearly to state the impossibility of attaining to knowledge by that method? The result of this method, as here authoritatively stated, is exactly described in the Scripture concerning our own time when it speaks of those who are "ever learning, and never able to come to the knowledge of the truth." 2 Tim. 3:7.

And, as if this writer should make it absolutely certain that only probability is the sole ground as to knowledge, which can ever be reached by this process, he really goes to the limit, and declares:—

> "Whether there ever existed on the earth such a person as Jesus, and what He experienced, are purely matters of historical evidence. And as everything that is a matter of evidence is a matter of probability, this must be also."

And where does the process finally land? What is its ultimate?

> "In a certain sense, the mind takes a leap into the dark: it literally passes *per saltum* [by a leap] from the realm of the known to the realm of the unknown."

The Place of the Bible in Education

And that is precisely where this process landed, and this was its ultimate, in ancient time, when at Athens, the fountain of this theory of education, they set up that monument of their ignorance, with its inscription, "TO THE UNKNOWN GOD."

But such is not the Christian process, nor is such the ultimate of the Christian process. In the Christian process, faith, which is the gift of God, accepts the truth of God; and thus in the mind and heart there is accomplished "a new creation." And the Creator in this new creation is God Himself, manifest through Jesus Christ our Lord, by the Holy Ghost. And in this, in the truest sense, the mind takes a leap, *not* "into the dark," but into the *light*. It truly, "literally, passes *per saltum*," *not* "from the realm of the known to the realm of the unknown," but from the realm of the unknown, the realm of ignorance, *to the realm of the known*, the realm of certain knowledge, even the knowledge of God. For we "know Him that is true, and we are in Him that is true, even in His Son Jesus Christ." 1 John 5:20.

Does this not show, then, that the world in this time, and by this means, has well-nigh reached the point which in ancient times it had attained when the world by wisdom knew not God, and was alienated from the life of God through its ignorance? And are we not therefore also in the time when again in the wisdom of God it shall please God "by the foolishness of preaching"—preaching the plain, simple, powerful gospel of Jesus Christ, the power of God and the wisdom of God—"to save them that *believe*"?

It is not true that "we have no other guide of life" than "the theory of probabilities." We have as the guide of life the certainty of truth, in the Word of God, as revealed in Jesus Christ, who Himself is "the Truth," through the Spirit of God, who is the very "Spirit of truth."

The Greek or "Scientific Method" Today.

It is not true that "even St. Paul himself could never have been certain that his explanation was more than a *probably* true one." For Paul's explanation was simply the preaching of the truth of God, derived from God. And not only Paul, but every other Christian, can be certain that the Word of God which he receives is certitude itself. And this certitude of the knowledge of truth he finds, not by reason guided by doubt, but *by revelation* to *faith*.

Whether there ever existed on earth such a person as Jesus, and what He experienced, are far more than merely "matters of historical evidence." And it is not true that "this must be" only a matter of probability. Every Christian knows that Christ lived in this world, that He was crucified that He died and rose again, and that He lives today. For every Christian knows by veritable knowledge of revelation and experience that Jesus is acquainted with every feature of his life in the flesh. Every Christian knows that Jesus was crucified; because he himself has been crucified with Him. Every Christian knows that Jesus died, for he himself has died with Him. Every Christian knows that Jesus rose from the dead, for he himself is risen with Him. And every Christian knows that Jesus, having risen from the dead lives today; for he himself lives with Him. Nor is this, in any sense, a guess, or a conjecture. It is a matter of very truth, in the certitude of knowledge.

Yet these simple things which every Christian knows, and which are but the A B C of Christianity, demonstrate that true Christianity, and even the professed *Christian* world today, are again set completely at opposites by the world's method of education. And these statements of the methods of education today, methods recognized even by the Protestant churches, show that instead of doubt being as is professed, "the pedagogue which leads to knowledge;" upon the authority of its own masters it is seen to be what it is in truth, the positive and chosen obstruction to all knowledge.

The Place of the Bible in Education

The *Outlook* presented it as a "problem of education" that "sorely needs to be taken up by our educators"—"the problem how religion can be preserved and promoted while education is being acquired." That is intensely true. But that problem never can be solved by any method of education of which doubt is in any degree an element; for doubt simply undermines all true religion. Faith, faith is the grand element of the true religion. It is only by an education in which faith is the beginning, the process, and the end that can ever be solved "the problem how religion can be preserved and promoted while education is being acquired." And this will do it; for this is Christian education.

Surely there is needed, and sorely needed, today, an educational reform. And, since the educational process of today is one in which doubt is the beginning the course, and the end, it is certain that the only true educational reform for today is one in which faith is the beginning, the course, and the end: and *that* faith, the faith of Jesus Christ, the faith which enables him who exercises it to comprehend, to understand, and to *know*, the truth, and only the truth—the truth as it is in Jesus.

In this it is not implied that in everything the Greeks were absolutely ignorant. There were many things that they learned as little children. There were many valuable facts of observation and experience that they knew. But in that which was their philosophy and their science, that which to them was preeminently wisdom and knowledge—in this they were absolutely ignorant. And this which to them was preeminently wisdom and knowledge, but which was in truth sheer confused ignorance—this was made to color all else and give to that the cast of ignorance. That which was as plainly true and easily to be understood as that A is A was not allowed to remain plain and simple knowledge, but it must first be *doubted*, and then through a process of hypothesis, premise, and conclusion, and then a

The Greek or "Scientific Method" Today.

new premise and conclusion, must be *reasoned* out to a final conclusion, and so "demonstrated." And thus that which was simple truth, and easily *known* if only believed, was overshadowed and utterly vitiated by their doubting and skeptical reasoning. Thus truth, faith, and knowledge were annihilated; and in their place was substituted falsity, doubt, and ignorance. They "changed the *truth* of *God* into a *lie*....And even as they did not *like* to *retain God* in their *knowledge*, God gave them over to a reprobate mind, to do those things which are not convenient; being filled with all unrighteousness." Rom. 1:25-29.

It is proper to inquire, What did Greek education accomplish for the Greeks, both directly and ultimately?

It can never be denied that *mentally* Greek education carried the Greeks to the highest point that has ever been attained in this world in education that was only human. The Greek language was developed by the Greek mind to the point wherein it excelled all other human language in its capacity and facility of expressing nice distinctions of thought. Of this it has been well said that "It traces with ease distinctions so subtle as to be lost in every other language. It draws lines where all other instruments of the reason only make blots."

In art, whether in sculpture or in architecture, the Greek education developed a standard that has never in the world been equaled. In physical culture, the development of the human form, also, Greek education attained the highest point that has ever been reached by any nation.

All this, Greek education undeniably did for the Greeks. But what did it do for them morally? Mental attainments that developed the fullest of all human languages, the most consummate skill in art, and the completest symmetry of the human form,—what did these attainments develop as to character? Everybody knows that the results in this respect could not be truly set down in this book,

The Place of the Bible in Education

without endangering its seizure by the police; and making the author liable to prosecution for circulating obscene literature.

It is impossible to walk amongst even the ruins of Greek art without being constantly offended with the perpetual portrayal and even the deification of drunkenness and lust, in the otherwise marvelous productions. In poetry, the highest form of that wonderful language, it is the same. The Greek poets developed a mythology in which the gods were portrayed as perpetually indulging the basest of human passions, and in which every idea of divinity was debased to the most degraded level of humanity.

And what did this education—the literature, the art, the physical culture, all that it produced—do for the Roman people when adopted by them? Deep-dyed as was the iniquity of Rome before she expanded into Greece, yet this iniquity was only given a deeper touch by that which was derived from Greece. Rom. 1:21–32 is a description of both. And the world knows the ultimate results—Greece and Rome perished so entirely that no part remained. The people of Greece today are not Greeks; the Greek nation today is not Greek. The people of Rome are not Romans. The world knows that Greece and Rome were annihilated by the flood of the barbarians of the wild forests of Germany. And when this flood of barbarism swept over Greece and Western Rome, the vices of the open life of even the highest classes were such as fairly to bring the blush to the iron cheeks of the Germans. A writer of the times declares:

> "We are worse than the barbarians and heathen. If the Saxon is wild, the Frank faithless, the Goth inhuman, the Alanian drunken, the Hun licentious, they are, by reason of their ignorance, far less punishable than we, who, knowing the commandments of God, *commit all* these crimes.

The Greek or "Scientific Method" Today.

"You, Romans, Christians, and Catholics, are defrauding your brethren, are grinding the face of the poor, are frittering away your lives for the impure and heathenish spectacles of the amphitheater, and wallowing in licentiousness and inebriety. The barbarians, meanwhile, heathen or heretics though they may be, however fierce toward us, are just and fair in their dealings with one another. The men of the same clan, and belonging to the same kin, love one another with true affection. The impurities of the theater are unknown amongst them. Many of their tribes are free from the taint of drunkenness: and among all except the Alanians and the Huns, *chastity is the rule*."

This being the ultimate result of Greek education both to Greece that originated it, and to Rome, both pagan and "Christian," that adopted it; and this result coming solely as the consequence of the essential immorality of that education; has demonstrated to the world forever the essential vanity and impotence of everything which claims to be education, in which character is not the one sole aim.

Annihilation being the result of Greek education to both Greek and Roman, what else than this can possibly be the result in a society or a nation which in education adopts the *method* which is Greek, and in its highest and most honorable course of education the *literature*, which is Greek and Roman?

Chapter 6.

The Separation of Christianity and the State.

THE Greek theory of education adopted by the apostate Church led to the union of Church and State, and the total ruin of the State. The principle of Christianity is the total separation of religion and the State. Christianity recognizes the right of the State to exist apart from the Church; and requires that the Church *must* exist apart from the State.

The Church and the State occupy two distinctly different realms. The realm of the Church is the realm of morals; the realm of the State is the realm of civics. The realm of the Church is the inner life of man, and the world to come: the realm of the State is the outward life of man, and the world that is.

The State rightly constituted, and abiding within its own realm, never can interfere with the affairs of the Church; and as a matter of fact, no State ever has interfered with the affairs of the Church, except when it went outside of its proper realm, and assumed to itself the garb of religion. The Church, abiding in its own realm, can never interfere in any way with the interests of the State; and, as a matter of fact, the Church has never done so, except where she left her own realm, ascended the throne of civil power, and presumed to wield the sword of the State.

The State, within its own realm, and for itself, has a right to establish a system of education, which in the nature of things must be only of this world. The Church, in her own realm, must maintain Christian education.

The Place of the Bible in Education

The State, in establishing and conducting such system of education as may seem to it best, can not ask that the Church shall abandon Christianity. The Church, in her own realm, in maintaining Christian education, can not ask that the State shall abandon such system of education as it may have adopted; and must not antagonize the State in its chosen system of education, any more than in any other affair or act of the State within its own realm.

The Government of the United States is the only one ever in the world that was founded upon the principle announced by Jesus Christ concerning civil government—the total separation of religion and the State.

> "No one thought of vindicating religion *for the conscience of the individual*, till a voice in Judea, breaking day for the greatest epoch in the life of humanity, by establishing a pure, spiritual, and universal religion for all mankind, enjoined to render to Caesar *only that which is Caesar's*. The rule was upheld during the infancy of the gospel for all men. No sooner was this religion adopted by the chief of the Roman Empire, than it was shorn of its character of universality, and enthralled by an unholy connection with the unholy State. And so it continued *till the new nation*—the least defiled with the barren scoffings of the eighteenth century, the most general believer in Christianity of any people of that age, the chief heir of the Reformation in its purest forms—*when it came to establish a government for the United States*, REFUSED TO TREAT FAITH AS A MATTER TO BE REGULATED BY A CORPORATE BODY, OR HAVING A HEADSHIP IN A MONARCH OR A STATE."—*George Bancroft.*

The men who made the United States, distinctly declared that in the matter of this fundamental principle of the separation of religion and the State, they were acting "upon the principles on which the gospel was first

The Separation of Christianity and the State.

propagated, and the Reformation from Popery carried on." They declared:

> "We hold it for a fundamental and undeniable truth, 'that religion, or the duty which we owe to our Creator, and the manner of discharging it, can be dictated only by reason and conviction, not by force or violence.' The religion, then, of every man must be left to the conviction and conscience of every man, and it is the right of every man to exercise it as these may dictate. This right is in its nature an inalienable right: it is inalienable, because the opinion of men depending only on the evidence contemplated in their own minds, can not follow the dictates of other men. It is inalienable, also, because what is here a right towards men is a duty towards the Creator.
>
> "It is the duty of every man to render to the Creator such homage, and such only, as he believes to be acceptable to Him. This duty is precedent, both in order of time, and in degree of obligation, to the claims of civil society. Before any man can be considered a member of civil society, he must be considered as a subject of the Governor of the universe; and if a member of a civil society who enters into any subordinate association must always do it with a reservation of his duty to the general authority, much more must every man who becomes a member of any particular civil society do it with a saving of his allegiance to the universal Sovereign. We maintain, therefore, that in matters of religion, no man's right is abridged by the institution of civil society; and that religion is wholly exempt from its cognizance."

In the course of its existence, the United States has developed and established a system of education. The principle upon which this system of education is founded is acknowledged to be, in this respect, the principle upon which the nation was founded—the separation of religion and the State: therefore religion must not be taught in the

The Place of the Bible in Education

State schools. This principle, though infringed in instances, has been generally adhered to on the part of the State. But THE CHURCH *has not adhered to this principle*: indeed, she has hardly recognized it at all. She has generally acquiesced in the State's adhering to the principle, and refusing to incorporate religion, or the religious method, in its system of education; but she has not at all adhered to the principle that *the Church must not adopt the secular method in education*. But this story is so well told by the United States Government itself that we need go no further in defining it.

In the Annual Report of the United States Commissioner of Education for the school year 1896–7, the United States Government has made perfectly clear the distinction between the secular method and the religious method in education: a distinction strictly in accordance with the principles of Christianity, and with the fundamental principles upon which the Government of the United States was founded.

First, as to the secular school: —

> "The secular school gives positive instruction. It teaches mathematics, natural science, history, and language. Knowledge of the facts can be precise, and accurate, and a similar knowledge of the principles can be arrived at. The self-activity of the pupil is before all things demanded by the teacher of the secular school. The pupil must not take things on authority; but, by his own activity, must test and verify what he has been told. He must trace out the mathematical demonstrations, and see their necessity. He must learn the method of investigating facts in the special provinces of science and history. The spirit of the secular school, therefore, comes to be an enlightening one, although not of the highest order. But its enlightenment tends to make trust in authority more and more difficult for the young mind."

The Separation of Christianity and the State.

Next, as to religious education: —

> "Religious education, it is obvious, in giving the highest results of thought and life to the young, must cling to the form of authority, and not attempt to borrow the methods of mathematics, science, and history from the secular school. Such borrowing will result only in giving the young people an overweening confidence in the finality of their own immature judgments. They will become conceited and shallow-minded. It is well that the child should trust his own intellect in dealing with the multiplication table and the rule of three. It is well that he should learn the rules and all the exceptions in Latin syntax, and verify them in the classic authors; but he must not be permitted to summon before him the dogmas of religion, and form pert conclusions regarding their rationality."

All this is an excellent reason as to why and how religion can not be taught in the public schools: why religious education can not be adopted by the State. And it gives just as excellent reason why the Church, in her education—"religious education"—can not even borrow, much less adopt, the methods of the secular school.

(a) "The self-activity of the pupil is before all things demanded by the teacher of the secular school." But in Christianity, instead of self-activity of the child or of the man, it is *self-surrender* and *self-emptying* that is before all things demanded. "If any man will be My disciple, let him deny himself, and take up his cross, and follow Me." "Let this mind be in you, which was also in Christ Jesus; who, being in the form of God, thought it not robbery to be equal with God," "but emptied Himself."

(b) In the secular school, "the pupil must not take things on authority." But in Christianity, in religious education, both the pupil and the teacher "must cling to the form of authority." This, because God is the Author of the religious sense in man, and of Christianity the only true complement of the religious sense; and the Word of God is the authority of Christianity. And God is supreme in everything. When He has spoken, that ends the matter. That is authority, the very ultimate of authority: not only because it is the Word of God, but because it is essential truth. And essential truth is the highest possible authority, and must be accepted as the authority which it is. Jesus Christ, who is the Truth, "spake as One having authority, and not as the scribes." His word was as from One having authority, not because he had any *position* of authority, but because of the essential truth which was expressed in the Word which He spake. All authority in heaven and on earth was given to Him, because He had all the truth in heaven and earth.

(c) "The spirit of the secular school," though "an enlightening one," yet is not "of the highest order;" while on the other hand, "religious education, it is obvious," gives "the highest results of thought and life."

(d) The enlightenment of the secular school "tends to make trust in authority more and more difficult for the young mind." Since, therefore, the enlightenment of the secular school tends to make trust in authority more and more difficult for the young mind: and since religious education must cling to the form of authority; it clearly follows that to adopt the spirit of the secular school, or to borrow the methods of the secular school, *in religious education*, is nothing less than to undermine the very citadel of religious education.

(e) It is therefore in perfect wisdom that the United States Government has given the counsel that in religious education there must be no "attempt to borrow the methods of mathematics, science, and history from the secular school." And this, for the further excellent reason that "such borrowing will result only in giving the young people an overweening confidence in the finality of their own immature judgments. They will become conceited and shallow-minded."

Every Christian desires that his children shall have a religious education. And surely no Christian who has any wish for the welfare of his children would consciously incorporate into their education that which would result in giving them an overweening confidence in the finality of their own immature judgments, and which will cause them to become conceited and shallow-minded. Surely, therefore, it has been in complete unconsciousness of the principles involved, and of the disastrous results incurred, that the Church leaders and teachers have, in education, taken precisely the course which the United States Government declares must not be taken: that is, the borrowing of the secular method in religious education. For that same report continues:—

> "With the spectacle of the systematic organization of the secular schools and the improved methods of teaching before them, the leaders in the *Church* have endeavored to perfect the methods of religious instruction of youth. They have met the following dangers which lay in their path: —
>
> "*First*, the danger of adopting methods of instruction in religion which were fit and proper only for secular instruction: *secondly*, the selection of religious matter for the course of study which did not lead in the most direct manner toward vital religion, although it would readily take on a pedagogic form.
>
> "Against *this danger of sapping, or undermining, all authority in religion*, BY THE INTRODUCTION OF THE METHODS OF THE SECULAR SCHOOL, which lay all stress on the self-activity of the child, the Sunday-school has not been sufficiently protected in the more recent years of its history. *Large numbers of religious teachers*, most intelligent and zealous in their

The Place of the Bible in Education

piety, *seek a more and more perfect adoption* of the secular school methods.

"On the other hand, the topics of religious instruction have been determined largely by the necessities of the secular school method. *That method is not adapted to teach mystic truth.* It seeks everywhere definite and especially mathematical results. *But these results,* although they are found everywhere in science and mathematics, *are the farthest possible from being like the subject matter of religion.* Hence, it has happened that in improving the methods of the Sunday-school, greater and greater attention has been paid to the history and geography of the Old Testament and less and less to the doctrinal matters of the New Testament."

(a) "The introduction of the methods of the secular school" in religious education incurs the danger "of sapping or undermining all authority in religion." And against this danger, even "the Sunday-school has not been sufficiently protected in the more recent years of its history." What, then, of the religious education of the children of Christians in the United States *outside of the Sunday-school?*

(b) "More and more perfect adoption of the secular school methods" has been sought even in the religious education *in the Sunday-school*. What, then, of the religious education of the children of Christians *apart* from the Sunday-school?

(c) "The topics of religious instruction, even in the Sunday-school, have been "determined largely by the necessities of the secular school method," which method "is not adapted to teach mystic truth;" and the results of which "are the farthest possible from being like the subject matter of religion." What, then, of the topics and methods in the religious instruction of the children of Christians apart from the Sunday-school?

The Separation of Christianity and the State.

When the professed Protestant Church has so far forsaken her own true Christian ground in education, and has so far adopted the topics and methods of secular education, has she not gone a long way in the course of the original apostasy in adopting the topics and method of secular education in that day? And in so doing, has not the Protestant Church in this day gone just that far on the way to the positive union of the Church and the State which resulted in the like course in ancient time? And with all this, how can the State here escape the certain ruin that must come from this apostasy and union of Church and State, as certainly as it came from that apostasy and union of Church and State in ancient time of which this is so exact a parallel and likeness?

Chapter 7.

The Bible's Right to Supreme Place in Christian Education.

FROM the evidence presented by the United States Government, it is certainly plain that, for the welfare of both the Church and the State, in this nation, there is demanded on the part of the professed Christian Church an education which shall be Christian. The document published by the United States Government, from which we have quoted, is nothing less than an appeal, a powerful appeal, that the Church leaders and teachers shall plant themselves upon the ground of a religious education which shall indeed be religious, instead of being a "more and more perfect adoption of the secular."

And when history has demonstrated that when the Church adopts the secular method in education it ends only in the ruin of the State, and the rise of the Church over that ruin into an ecclesiastical world-power, a theocratical world kingdom, of the most desperately oppressive character of all powers that ever were on earth: then is it not for the highest possible welfare of the State, and of human society as a whole, that the Church shall be called back from this secular ground, to her own fair realm of the Christian religion in its purity and its sincerity, and to the education which is wholly becoming to her as the true and sincere Christian Church?

This education, to be Christian, must find its spring in the Word of God alone. That Word must be the basis, the inspiration, and the guide in every line of study. And there

The Place of the Bible in Education

must be such a true faith and such perfect confidence in that Word as the Word of God, in which are hid all the treasures of wisdom and knowledge; and such a profound study of that Word, illuminated by the Divine Spirit; that it shall be clearly seen that truly "There is no subtlety in grammar, neither in logic, nor in any other science that can be named, but that it is found in more excellent degree in the Scriptures." This will make her that she shall be indeed the light of the world.

For anybody to profess to believe the Bible for what it is,—the Word of God,—and at the same time not allow that the Bible must be the leading book in all education, are two things that will not hold together at all.

The Bible claims for itself that it is the Word of God. It comes to men as the Word of God. If it is not accepted and held as the Word of God, it is no more than any other peculiarly national book. To believe the Bible, is to accept it as the Word of God; for that is the only claim that the Bible makes for itself. Not to accept the Bible as the Word of God, is not to believe *the Bible* at all.

But how shall men know that it is the Word of God? This is the question that thousands of people ask. They ask, "What proof is there, where is the evidence, that it is the Word of God?"

There is evidence,—evidence that every man can have,—evidence that is convincing and satisfactory. Where is it, then? Let us see.

Being the Word of God, where alone could evidence be found that it is such? Where should we expect to find such evidence?

Is there any one of greater knowledge than God, or of greater authority than He, of whom we may inquire?—Certainly not. For whoever God may be, there

The Bible's Right to Supreme Place in Christian Education.

can be no higher authority, there can be none of greater knowledge.

Suppose, then, we were to ask God whether this is His Word. And suppose that, apart from the Bible, He should tell us, in so many words, "The Bible is My word," we should even then have only *His word* for it.

But *we have that already*, over and over; so that even then we should have no more evidence than we now have in abundance: and the evidence would be in nowise different; for it would be the evidence of His word, and that we already have.

Therefore the truth is that the Word of God bears *in itself* the evidence that it is the Word of God. And it is impossible that it could be otherwise.

If God had never yet spoken a word to the human family, and should this day send a message to all people at once, and in their own native tongues, that word, being the word of God, would *have* to bear in itself the evidence of its being the word of God; for the people could not possibly inquire of any other, because there is no person whose knowledge or authority is superior to this. And that word, bearing in itself the evidence of its being the word of God, all the people could obtain this evidence by accepting it *as the word of God*. Each one who did this would know it to be the word of God; for he would have the evidence *in the word*, and by *accepting it,* also *in himself*.

This is precisely the position that the Bible occupies toward the people of this world. It comes as the Word of God. As such, it must bear the evidence in itself; for there can be no higher, no better, evidence. Whoever receives it as the Word of God receives in *it* and in *himself* the evidence that it is the Word of God. And so it is written, "When ye received the Word of God which ye heard of us, ye received it *not as the word of men*, but as it is in truth, the

The Place of the Bible in Education

Word of God, which *effectually worketh also* in you that believe." 1 Thess. 2:13.

"Again, a new commandment I write unto you, which thing is true *in Him and in you*." 1 John 2:8.

And again: "My doctrine is not Mine, but His that sent Me. If any man will [is willing to] do His will, *He shall know* of the doctrine, *whether it be of God*, or whether I speak of Myself." John 7:16 , 17.

Thus he who accepts the Word as the Word of God finds the evidence that it is the Word of God. He who will not accept the Word can not have the evidence. In rejecting the Word, he rejects the evidence; because the evidence is in the Word.

To make this yet plainer, if possible, especially to those who do not know that the Bible is the Word of God, we may, for the sake of the case, suppose that the Bible were not the Word of God, and that the God of the Bible were not the true God. Suppose, then, that we should find the true God, and ask Him whether the Bible is the Word of God; and suppose He should say, "It is not the Word of God." We should then have only *His word*; and the only way that we could know whether or not this answer were true would be by believing it, by accepting it as the word of God.

So, then, the only possible way in which any person could surely know that the Bible is *not* the Word of God would be by the Word of God. And even though he had the Word of God to this effect, the only way that be could be sure of it—the only *evidence* he could have—would be *by believing* that Word.

But there is *no word* of God that the Scriptures are *not* the Word of God; while there *is the Word of God* that the Scriptures *are* the Word of God. That Word of God bears in itself the evidence that it is the Word of God: and every

The Bible's Right to Supreme Place in Christian Education.

soul who will receive it as it is, will have the evidence. The evidence will be plain to him who believes the Word.

The Bible, then, being the Word of God, is supreme knowledge and supreme authority upon every subject that is true. There can not be any truer knowledge than that of God: there can not be any higher authority than that of the Word of God. As certainly, therefore, as the Bible is an educational book at all, so certainly is it the supreme educational Book.

And the Bible is educational only. The Author of it presents Himself as the Teacher of men: "I am the Lord thy God which teacheth thee to profit." "And they shall be all taught of God."

He by whom that Word came, and who is indeed the Word of God, calls all men to Him to learn: "Come unto Me, all ye....Learn of Me." In calling all men to Him to learn of Him, in that very thing He presents Himself as the Teacher of all. He is the great Teacher "sent from God."

And these two Supreme Teachers have given the Holy Spirit, and Themselves in Him, to be the Teacher of men. "The Comforter, which is the Holy Ghost, whom the Father will send in My name, He shall teach you all things"—not all things good, bad, and indifferent; not all things speculative, conjectural, and false; but all things that are *true*: not false science, but true science; not false philosophy, but true philosophy. For He is the Spirit only of *truth*. He is a guide only into *truth*: and "He will guide you into *all* truth." And He teaches only the Word of God: "He shall teach you all things, and bring all things to your remembrance, whatsoever *I have said* unto you." "He shall not speak of [from] Himself; but whatsoever *He shall hear*, that shall He speak."

The Holy Spirit being the Representative of the Godhead to men, being the Spirit of *Truth*, teaches only in and through and by means of the Word of God, as that

The Place of the Bible in Education

Word is the *truth*. The Godhead, therefore, in the Holy Spirit, is the Supreme Instructor; and the Word of God is the basis of all true instruction. To the Bible, therefore, being the Word of God and being instruction from the Lord, belongs, *by divine right*, the place of first consideration in all Christian, in all true, education.

What kind of treatment, then, is it of the Father, and of the Son, and of the Holy Spirit—what kind of treatment is it of the Godhead, *by Christians*, when they put men before the Godhead, and the books of men, the books of even pagan and infidel men, before the Book of God, in education? Is this fair? Is it reverent? Is it of faith? Is it Christian?

To the Bible by divine right belongs the first consideration and the supreme place in all Christian education. To the Bible also *by the very philosophy of education itself* belongs the first consideration and the supreme place in Christian education.

The Bible should be the first thing in every line of study, for the reason that is expressed in a saying familiar to all: First impressions are most lasting. For this reason the Bible should be the source of the first instruction that the child receives in the world; and, as everybody is a child in the beginning of every line of study, the Bible should be the first of all things in all studies.

It is the truth that when a person lives, and a few do live, to such an age that the life simply fades out because of age, the last thing that such a person thinks of is the first thing that he ever learned. This may be said again, for it is a *principle* of education: The first thing that is ever fixed upon a person's mind is the last thing that that mind dwells upon, if the life of that person is completed and simply fades out in old age.

A notable instance of this is William Ewart Gladstone, the great English statesman, who died in 1898. He died a very old man. As his life was fading out indeed, it was

The Bible's Right to Supreme Place in Christian Education.

noticed that he was saying over and over again the Lord's prayer *in French*. That excited some query: as he was an Englishman, why should he be saying the Lord's prayer in *French*? Inquiries were made, and it was learned that when he was a little child, he was in charge of a French nurse, and that that French nurse was a Christian, and had taught him the Lord's prayer in her native language. And as that happened to be the first thing that was fixed upon his mind, it was the last thing that was dwelt upon by his mind as it faded out in death.

Now, if that nurse had not been a Christian, and had taught that child, "Hi, diddle, diddle, the cat's in the fiddle," it would have worked precisely the same way, and *that* would have been the last thing that he would have spoken on his death-bed. If she had taught him Æsop's fables or fairy tales instead of the Lord's prayer, these would have been the last things that he would have murmured as his mind faded away.

Another, who was personally known to the writer, died at a little past ninety-six years of age. The Lord's prayer was also one of the last things that that person repeated. Another thing she did in the last days of her life was to count—one, two, three, four, five, six, seven, and so on up to ten, *but not beyond*—just as a little child learns to count. So that mind, in its last hours, was dwelling on the things of her first hours of conscious memory—the things that were first fixed in her mind.

How beautiful it is that the last thought of a mind fading out in death is the thought of God in His Word! How aptly in the resurrection will the first thought take up the connection! This is enough to illustrate the principle that is the basis of the philosophy of using the Bible as the first thing in all Christian education.

This, all will admit, is all well enough in the case of the child, who is learning the first things. Yet it is no more necessary there than it is everywhere else; for every one is a child, an infant, in the things that he is first learning. If you or I were to begin to study any new language, we should be altogether babes in that language. We know nothing at all there: there is not a thought in the language that is ours; not a word in the language that can possibly convey a thought.

To illustrate: suppose you would learn the German language, and that the first words you ever learn are these: "*Im anfang war das Wort.*" Then the first *thought* which ever enters your mind in the German language is, "In the beginning was the Word." Then, having *learned* this, wherever after that, as long as you live, you meet the word *anfang*, that word will unfailingly recall the expression, "*Im anfang war das Wort*," and the *thought*, "In the beginning was the Word."

Or suppose it be Greek, and the first words that you ever learn in it are the same: "Εν ἀρχῃ ἦν ὅ λόγος" "*En arche en ho Logos.*" The word *arche* means "the beginning," and the word *logos* means "the word." "In the beginning was the Word." Then, having *learned* this, wherever you meet either the word *arche* or *Logos*, instantly occurs the thought first lodged in your mind with the passage, "In the beginning was the Word."

But suppose you unfortunately fall into the hands of a teacher with whom the Bible is not supreme, and therefore is not the first and most important book in every line of study. Suppose that the first words in the language that he gives to you are from some fairy story, some fable, some novel, some play, or from *any* other source than the Bible. When you learn those words, you receive the *thought* expressed by the words. And having learned *that*, then afterward, when you meet those same words in the Bible, instantly and irresistibly your mind will revert to that first thought in those words, and the clear rays of light and

The Bible's Right to Supreme Place in Christian Education.

truth in the words of the Bible will be clouded and confused by being mixed up with that fairy scene, or whatever it was that was first associated in your mind with those words. Then your very study of the Bible will be hindered, and you will be crippled, by such a bad beginning in the new language. On the other hand, when you begin right, with the words of the Bible and the thoughts of God first, then if, for any purpose, you should find it necessary to read these other books, you will find the precious light and wisdom and strength of the thoughts of God constantly recurring and abiding with you, guiding you in the way of truth, and guarding you against that which is false.

In illustration, an actual occurrence can be cited: A few years ago the author of this book was passing through a high school, in which persons of another language were taking first lessons in English. The students had just gone from the room, and lying on the desks were their books of study in English; some of them open at the latest lesson. And the subject of that lesson was "The Mischievous Monkey." Those students were taking their first lessons in a new language. The first and only thoughts that they were getting in that language were thoughts about a mischievous monkey. When they had studied that piece clear through so that they could intelligently read it in English, a large proportion of what they knew, and of the thoughts that they were able to think, in English were solely concerning a mischievous monkey.

In the account of that mischievous monkey words were used that are frequently met in the Bible; because they were common English words. Suppose then that those students should soon afterward turn to the Bible in English, and there meet some of these same words: every time they should meet one of those words, there would be that mischievous monkey obtruding himself upon, and rollicking among, the thoughts of the Word of God. That

The Place of the Bible in Education

is as certain as that those students received the thoughts about that mischievous monkey as their first thoughts in English. And that would also be a positive hindrance to their ever getting from the Word of God in English the clear, pure thoughts of that Word.

What a lasting injury, then, it is to students, and especially the young: what an imposition upon them: when they are kept for years in the wild, foolish, false, and wicked imaginings of pagan poets, philosophers, or dramatists, or even the writings of historians, before they are qualified to read New Testament Greek or Bible Latin! Is a mind whose whole warp and woof in Greek is pagan, the better qualified to understand and appreciate Christian Greek? Is a mind that has roamed from one to three years all over Gaul, amid the barbarities of Caesar and the Gauls, or that has dwelt all its Greek or Latin life in the pagan miasma of Homer or Virgil,—is such a mind the better prepared to read in Latin, to Christian profit, the gospel of John or the epistles of Paul? Are paganism and barbarism an essential basis for Christianity? Are pagan thoughts and heathen conceptions an essential antecedent to Christian thoughts and divine conceptions?

If not, why do teachers who consider themselves, and expect others to consider them, *Christians*, cause their students of Greek, or Latin, or any other language, to build up their minds in that language wholly of pagan material, and that from one to three years, before they are expected, or given any chance, to form their minds of the Lord's thoughts—the perfectly good, the perfectly pure, the perfectly true?

For all practical purposes, the mind is composed of thoughts. The object of study is to build up the mind, to obtain thoughts—knowledge. What, then, can be the object of professed Christian teachers in having students study pagan Greek and pagan Latin first of all? Whatever

The Bible's Right to Supreme Place in Christian Education.

their object, the certain result is to build up the minds of the students in paganism and of paganism. What the mind is, the man is. And when the mind is pagan, the man is pagan; and if the mind is mostly, or even partly, pagan, then the man is mostly' or partly pagan.

But is it the God-given task, or responsibility, of Christian teachers to cause students to become even in any degree whatever, pagan? The only possible answer is, No. Then what Christian teacher can ever put any pagan book into the hands of any student as a text-book, or as a book for study at all?

This is not to say that no other book but the Bible can ever be read or studied in a foreign language; but it *is* to say that no other book should ever be read or studied in any foreign language until that language has been *learned* from the Bible, and until the Bible can readily be read at sight in that language. When this has been, and can be, done by a person, then that person can read with perfect safety, and to profit, any other book in that language which he may find it necessary to consult.

Which is the better, which affords the better prospect to the mind and soul—to begin a study in such a way that wherever the person shall go afterward in that field, the thought of God shall accompany him; or to begin in such a way that paganism, infidelity, or worldliness, shall be first in all the field, even to the overshadowing of the Word of God when it is studied?—To ask that question is certainly to answer it in all Christian minds.

It is therefore perfectly plain that, both by divine right and by the simple philosophy of education, to the Bible belongs the first consideration and the supreme place in all Christian education. What Christian teacher, then, can be loyal to the Godhead in putting any book but the Bible first of all into the thoughts of any student on any subject?

Chapter 8.

The Education of Daniel.

THE Bible is treated fairly, and is given its true place in education, only when it is confidently held to be distinctly an educational book as such: only when it is held to have clearly an educational purpose, and to be positively committed to the principle of a complete education as such.

That the Bible is all this is abundantly proved by the contents of the Book itself. In order to cause this to be seen most fully, and yet to do it in the briefest space, we shall approach the subject through the book that is in more than one point a pivotal book in the Bible—the book of Daniel.

The book of Daniel was written especially for the last days; for when Daniel came to explain to King Nebuchadnezzar the great things of the king's dream, he said that God "maketh known to the King Nebuchadnezzar what shall be in the latter days." Dan. 2:28. In explaining to Daniel the things revealed, the angel said that he was giving understanding of what should befall God's people "in the latter days." Dan. 10:14. And when the writing of the book was finished, Daniel was commanded to "shut up the words, and seal the book, even to the time of the end" (Dan. 12:4); and was then told, "Go thy way, Daniel; for the words are closed up and sealed till the time of the end" (Verse 9).

The book of Daniel, then, being specifically designed for the last days, contains principles, as well as prophecies, which are of special importance, and have a special bearing, in the last days; and not the least of these are the principles of education. These principles are given to save the people of the world in the last days from calamities and destruction of which those that came upon Babylon are but a feeble representation. To ignore these principles, given especially for this time, is but to court a destruction as much more dreadful than that other as world-wide destruction and eternal ruin are greater than local destruction and temporal ruin.

When Nebuchadnezzar king of Babylon captured Jerusalem the first time, "the king spake unto Ashpenaz the master of his eunuchs, that he should bring certain of the children of Israel and of the king's seed and of the princes; children in whom was no blemish, but well favored, and skillful in all wisdom, and cunning in knowledge, and understanding science, and such as had ability in them to stand in the king's palace, and *whom they might teach the learning* and the tongue of the Chaldeans." Dan. 1:3, 4.

"No blemish" and "well favored." This would require that they should be physically sound, well built, and symmetrical.

The words translated "wisdom," "knowledge," and "science," in verse 4—Hebrew *daath*, *madda*, and *chokmah*—are closely related, though the second is an extension of the first, and the third an extension of the second.

The word translated "wisdom" signifies "knowledge, understanding, and intelligence." It implies the faculty to discern what is valuable knowledge, and the ability and capacity to acquire such knowledge.

The word translated "knowledge" relates to "the mind or thought," and implies knowledge acquired by thinking and application.

The Education of Daniel.

The word translated "science" signifies "skill, dexterity, sagacity, shrewdness, ability to judge;" and is well translated in our word "science," which signifies "skillful in knowledge." It implies a selected and systematized knowledge.

Therefore the requirement of King Nebuchadnezzar in the selecting of these youth was that they should be physically sound and symmetrically built; and that, mentally, they should be —

1. Skillful in discerning what is valuable knowledge, and skillful in the ability to acquire such knowledge;

2. Cunning in the acquisition of knowledge by thinking and application; and —

3. Understanding how to correlate, classify, and systematize the knowledge which they had the faculty to discern was valuable knowledge, and which they were cunning in gathering.

And they must have *"ability"* in all these things. What they knew was not to be mere head-knowledge; but they must have the faculty of observation and adaptation so trained that what they had learned could be practically applied in their experience in every-day affairs. They were to have such ability, such every-day common sense, as would enable them to use their knowledge to practical advantage in the common things of daily life, so that they would be practical men wherever they were; so that they could adapt themselves to any circumstances or situation, and be the master and not the slave of either circumstances or situation.

From the specifications distinctly made in the scripture, and from the close and thorough examination that must be passed, it is certain that all that we have outlined was comprehended in the requirements of the king respecting the youth who were to be chosen. And this is no small

The Place of the Bible in Education

tribute to the educational ideas of King Nebuchadnezzar. Indeed, his views of education, as shown in this verse of the Bible, were, for all practical purposes, far in advance of the educational system that prevails today, even in the leading colleges and universities of the United States.

Yet Daniel, Hananiah, Mishael and Azariah were able successfully to pass such an examination. Where, then, did they get such an education, being, as they were, but mere youth? The answer to this question is worth having. Besides, we need it just now; for all this was written especially for the last days.

Where, then, did Daniel and his three companions obtain the education which enabled them successfully to pass the examination required by King Nebuchadnezzar? Where did they obtain an education which made them "skillful in all wisdom, and cunning in knowledge, and understanding science;" and which gave them "ability" in all these things?—Without hesitation it can be answered, In a "school of the prophets," the divinely-established schools in Israel. There was at that time a "college," or "school of the prophets," in Jerusalem. For in the eighteenth year of Josiah, king of Judah, which was only fifteen years before the captivity of Daniel, there is the clear record of such a school in Jerusalem.

In the eighteenth year, of Josiah, while at his command the temple was being cleansed and repaired from the abominations of Manasseh and Amen, a copy of the Pentateuch, or "book of the law of the Lord of Moses," was found by Hilkiah the priest. Hilkiah "delivered the book to Shaphan" the scribe; and "Shaphan carried the book to the king," and "read it before the king." "And it came to pass, when the king had heard the words of the law, that he rent his clothes," and commanded Hilkiah the priest, and Shaphan the scribe, and others, "Go, inquire of the Lord

The Education of Daniel.

for me, and for them that are left in Israel and in Judah, concerning the words of the book that is found."

"And Hilkiah, and they that the king had appointed, *went to Huldah the prophetess*....Now *she dwelt* in Jerusalem *in the college* [margin, "*in the school*"]; and they spoke to her to that effect."

Here was, in Jerusalem, a college, or school, in which "*dwelt*" the prophetess. This at once shows this school to have been a school of the prophets; because that which gave to those schools the name schools of the Prophets was the fact that a prophet dwelt with the school, and was, under God, the head of the school. This fact is revealed in the two other instances in which they are mentioned: in 1 Sam. 19:20 "the company of the prophets" was seen, and "Samuel standing *as appointed* over them." In 2 Kings 6:1–6 we meet again "the sons of the prophets," and Elisha the prophet is dwelling with them; for they said to Elisha, "The place where we dwell *with thee* is too strait for us."

Thus we find three schools of the prophets in three widely-separated ages,—the age of Samuel, the age of Elisha, and the age of Josiah,—and in each instance a prophet is dwelling in the school. These three passages were written to give us information as to the schools of the prophets. They show why these schools were called schools of the prophets. They show also that the college, or school, in Jerusalem, in which dwelt Huldah the prophetess, was a school of the prophets as certainly as was the school where dwelt Elisha the prophet or Samuel the prophet.

It was, then, in a school of the prophets, in the Lord's school, and in the system of education of the Lord's designing, where Daniel and his three companions obtained the education of which we read in Dan. 1:4,—the education which made them "skillful in all wisdom, and cunning in knowledge, and understanding science," and

The Place of the Bible in Education

which gave to them such "ability" in all these that they were able to pass successfully the examination required for entrance into the royal university of Babylon.

Chapter 9.

What Was Taught in the Schools of the Prophets.

WHAT was taught in the schools of the prophets? To know this is important, not only for its own sake: but because, when we know this, we know what should be taught in the Lord's schools always. These things are in the Bible. They were written for our learning. And being in the book of Daniel, they are written especially for our instruction and admonition "upon whom the ends of the world are come." In this chapter we shall have space only to discover and enumerate these studies. What each subject involved will be studied afterward.

Daniel and his three companions were "skillful in all wisdom, and cunning in knowledge, and understanding science." This education was acquired in the college, or school of the prophets in Jerusalem. This, therefore, certifies that *wisdom*, *knowledge*, and *science* were taught in those schools.

Another thing that was taught there was *music*, instrumental as well as vocal. This we know from the fact that the first time that we meet any of the students of such a school, they have "a psaltery, and a tabret, and a pipe, and a harp, *before them;*" and they were playing with such spirit, and with such power in the Spirit, that the man who then personally met them was drawn to God and converted. Thus all the circumstances show that this was trained, harmonious music, played by the students of this school.

The Place of the Bible in Education

And this is plain evidence that music was taught in the schools of the prophets.

Another thing that was taught there was *work*, or "manual training" as it would be called today. This we know from the record of these schools in the time of Elisha: "And the sons of the prophets said unto Elisha, Behold now, the place where we dwell with thee is too strait for us. Let us go, we pray thee, unto Jordan, and take thence every man a beam, and let us make us a place there, where we may dwell. And he answered, Go ye. And one said, Be content, I pray thee, and go with thy servants. And he answered, I will go. So he went with them. And when they came to Jordan, they cut down wood." 2 Kings 6:1–4.

This shows that in those schools, *work* was taught and the love of it; because when the school building became too small for the attendance, the *students themselves* suggested that *they themselves* should build the new and larger house that was needed. There was no thought of hiring other people to do the work, nor of letting it by contract. No; they themselves said, "*Let us* go,...and *let us* make us a place."

They were also so in love with work that they would borrow tools with which to work; for when one of the axes flew off the handle and into the river, as one of the students was chopping, he exclaimed to Elisha, "Alas, master! for it was *borrowed*."

More than this, even the principal of the school—Elisha—went with them to the work, and *joined with them in the work*; for he was among those who were chopping on the bank of the river when the ax flew into the water.

All this shows, as plainly as needs to be shown, that work and the love of it, real industry, was taught in the schools of the prophets—the Lord's schools of ancient time.

What Was Taught in the Schools of the Prophets.

Another thing that was taught there was *temperance*—healthful living. This is shown by the fact that Daniel and his companions refused the king's dainties and royal food, and the wine which he drank, and *asked* for a simple fare, a vegetarian diet. Dan. 1:5, 12–16. That they were *taught* this in the school of the prophets which they attended is plain from the fact that this was a thoroughly grounded principle with them. And that such was the diet in the schools of the prophets is taught by the fact that in that school, in the time of Elisha, even when "there was a *dearth* in the land," Elisha, giving directions to prepare food, said, "Set on the great pot, and seethe pottage." And in following this direction, "one went out into the field to gather *herbs*." 2 Kings 4:38, 39. When herbs were gathered in response to the ordinary direction to prepare food, and this when "there was a dearth in the land," surely this is strong evidence that a vegetarian diet was the regular diet in the school. This is confirmed by the further fact that "there came a man from Baal-shalisha, and brought the man of God bread of the first-fruits, twenty loaves of barley, and full ears of corn in the husk thereof. And he [Elisha] said, Give unto the people, that they may eat." Verse 42. Here was a man bringing a present of provisions to the principal of the school, and he brought only food from the vegetable kingdom.

All this is evidence that a vegetarian diet was the diet of the students and teachers in the schools of the prophets; that this temperate way of living was a part of the instruction; and that temperance was so inculcated as to become a living principle in the lives of the students.

Another thing taught there was *law*—statutes, justice, and judgment. This was directly commanded to be taught: "Behold, I have taught you statutes and judgments, even as the Lord my God commanded me, *that ye should do so* in the land whither ye go to possess it. Keep therefore and do them; for this is your wisdom and your understanding in the sight of the nations, which shall hear all these statutes, and say, Surely this great nation is a wise and understanding people.... What nation is there so great, that hath statutes and judgments so righteous as all this law, which I set before you this day? Only take heed to thyself, and keep thy soul diligently, lest thou forget the things which thine eyes have seen, and lest they depart from thy heart in all the days of thy life; but teach them thy sons, and thy sons' sons." Deut. 4:5–9. "Justice, justice, shalt thou follow." Deut. 16:20, margin.

Another thing taught there, and this "*specially*," was *morals*; for after urging upon them the obligation to teach carefully and diligently the statutes and judgments of the Lord, he commanded them to teach to their sons and their sons' sons, "specially," the ten commandments which they heard, said he, "the day that thou stoodest before the Lord thy God in Horeb, when the Lord said unto me, Gather Me the people together, and I will make them hear My words, that they may learn to fear Me all the days that they shall live upon the earth, and *that they may teach their children*.... And the Lord spake unto you out of the midst of the fire; ye heard the voice of the words, but saw no similitude; only ye heard a voice. And He declared unto you His covenant, which He commanded you to perform, even ten commandments; and He wrote them upon two tables of stone."

Another thing taught there was *history*: "When thy son asketh thee in time to come, saying, What mean the testimonies, and the statutes, and the judgments, which the Lord our God hath commanded you? then thou shalt say unto thy son, We were Pharaoh's bondmen in Egypt; and the Lord brought us out of Egypt with a mighty hand; and the Lord showed signs and wonders, great and sore, upon Egypt, upon Pharaoh, and upon all his household, before our eyes." Deut. 6:20–22. This study was not confined to the history of the deliverance from Egypt; it embraced all

What Was Taught in the Schools of the Prophets.

as it was given in the sacred writings. We know that this history was one of the studies of Daniel; for the form of government, having three presidents, one of whom was chief, which was introduced by Daniel as prime minister in the days of Darius the Mede, was adopted literally from the records of Israel as to the government of David.

Yet another thing taught there was *poetry*. This was an essential accompaniment of the teaching of music, and the songs of worship of which their music was composed. With all this, of course, the fundamentals of knowledge, reading and writing and numbers, were taught.

We find, then, that the teaching in the schools of the prophets embraced at least the following studies:—

1. Wisdom,
2. Knowledge,
3. Science,
4. Manual labor,
5. Music,
6. Poetry,
7. Temperance,
8. Morals,
9. Law,
10. History,
11. Reading,
12. Writing,
13. Numbers

But the one greatest thing over all, in all, and through all, in the Lord's schools was the pervading presence of the divine Teacher, the Holy Spirit. In the schools of the prophets the Spirit of God was the one all-pervading influence, the one great prevailing power. The first time we

The Place of the Bible in Education

meet one of these schools is in 1 Sam. 10:5–12, when Saul came "to the hill of God," and met "a company of prophets coming down" with instruments of music, and prophesying. "And the Spirit of God came upon him," and "God gave him another heart;" he was turned "into another man," and "he prophesied among the prophets."

That this should occur in the case of such a man as Saul was so great a wonder that the people of Israel were astonished at it to such an extent that henceforth it became a proverb in Israel, "Is Saul also among the prophets?"

Yet this was but the usual degree of the manifestation of the Spirit in the school. For we find after this that Saul, by disobedience to God and jealousy of David, had separated himself from the Spirit, and was constantly seeking to kill David, and David escaped, and fled, and "came to Samuel to Ramah," and "he and Samuel went and dwelt in Naioth. And it was told Saul, saying, Behold, David is at Naioth in Ramah." This was where there was a school of the prophets. "And Saul sent messengers to take David: and when they saw the company of the prophets prophesying, and Samuel standing as appointed over them, the Spirit of God was upon the messengers of Saul, and they also prophesied. And when it was told Saul, he sent other messengers, and they prophesied likewise."

When Saul saw that his first messengers had yielded, of course he sent the second time such ones as he supposed would not yield. And when he found that they also had yielded, he determined to trust no more messengers—he would go himself. Therefore in his wrathful determination "went he also to Ramah," and demanded, "Where are Samuel and David? And one said, Behold, they be at Naioth in Ramah. And he went thither to Naioth in Ramah: and the Spirit of God was upon him also, and he went on, and prophesied."

What Was Taught in the Schools of the Prophets.

All this shows, and it was written to tell to us, that the Holy Spirit was so fully manifested that stern, hard-hearted, and even exceptionally unspiritual men were melted and subdued by His gracious influence whenever they came in contact with the school. It shows also that the Spirit of God in these schools manifested Himself in prophesyings. Thus it was the Spirit of prophecy that pervaded and controlled the school. "The Spirit of prophecy" is "the testimony of Jesus" (Rev. 19:10), in counsel and instruction. Thus Jesus Christ Himself, by the Spirit of prophecy, was the real Head of the schools of the prophets.

And all this is to teach to us now, for our own time, that in the Lord's schools, the Spirit of prophecy, the testimony of Jesus, must be the great guide and instructor, and that the Spirit of God is to be courted until He shall become the all-pervading influence and the all-controlling power in every school established in the name of the Lord.

These things are written in the Bible for us. They center and are emphasized in the book of Daniel specially for the last days. We are now in the last days. The instruction given, the course of study in the schools of the prophets, is instruction for the Lord's schools for all time. This is the instruction that belongs today in every school that makes any pretensions to being a Christian school.

Chapter 10.

The Study of Wisdom.

DANIEL, while yet a mere youth, was "skillful in all wisdom." This was the leading part of his education.

What is wisdom? whence comes it? how is it attained? and what relation does it bear to education in general?

"Where shall wisdom be found? and where is the place of understanding? Man knoweth not the price thereof; neither is it found in the land of the living. The depth saith, It is not in me; and the sea saith, It is not with me. It can not be gotten for gold, neither shall silver be weighed for the price thereof. . .

"Whence then cometh wisdom? and where is the place of understanding? Seeing it is hid from the eyes of all living, and kept close from the fowls of the air. Destruction and death say, We have heard the fame thereof with our ears.

"*God* understandeth the way thereof, and *He* knoweth the place thereof....When He made a decree for the rain, and a way for the lightning of the thunder; then did He see it, and declare it; He prepared it, yea, and searched it out. And unto man *He* said, Behold, *the fear of the Lord*, THAT IS WISDOM; and to depart from evil is understanding." Job 28:12–28. And "the Lord giveth wisdom." Prov. 2:6.

It is certain, then, that *the fear of the Lord* was an essential part of the education in the schools of the prophets. Since only God knoweth what is truly wisdom, and since He is the Giver of it, this, in itself, required that the revelation which God had given of Himself should be studied, that they might truly know the true God and His attributes. For they could not fear—reverence—Him unless they knew Him. And in studying the revelation which the Lord had given, this, of itself, was the study of the sacred writings,—the books of Moses and the writings of the other prophets.

As "the fear of the Lord is the beginning of knowledge," it is certain that wisdom was the leading subject of study in the schools of the prophets. It preceded every other study. More than this, it not only preceded every other study; but it was the leading element, the guiding principle, *in* every other study. And as the knowledge of God is essential to the fear of God, and the certain knowledge of God is attained only by revelation that He has given of Himself and of His attributes, it is certain that *the Holy Scriptures* were the essential basis of all studies, the guide in every course of investigation, and the ultimate test of every inquiry.

Wisdom is "the fear of the Lord," and "the fear of the Lord is the beginning of knowledge." All that any person can possibly know in this world *without* the fear of the Lord will, in "a little time," vanish forevermore: while he who knows the fear of the Lord will abide forevermore. That which he learns in accordance with the fear of the Lord will also, with him, abide forevermore; and forevermore there is open to him the wide universe, with all its possibilities for the increase of knowledge. Thus he who has the fear of the Lord has also, *in that*, for all eternity, all things else: while whatever else he might have *without the fear of God*, he would not really have even that; because in a little while all that, *with himself*, must vanish. Thus in the very nature of things, the fear of the Lord is the most important of all things, and is therefore properly the beginning of knowledge as well as of everything else.

The Study of Wisdom.

It must be borne in mind, too, that the fear of the Lord was distinctly taught there. The teaching with respect to the Lord was not merely in the teaching of doctrines, or subjects, in the Scriptures; it was not in the teaching of theology, or things *about* the Lord. The fear of the Lord itself, as a distinctive thing in the individual experience, was taught. The students were instructed as to what the fear of the Lord is, how to approach unto Him, how to pray to Him, how to submit themselves to Him, how to commune with Him, how to court His Holy Spirit, how to be led of the Spirit, how to live with God, how to walk with Him, how to have the Lord dwell in their lives, how to know that they were ever in His presence, how to have Him their companion in everything that they did in their daily lives,—in short, how to glorify God in body, soul, and spirit, in every thought and word and deed.

All this is the teaching of wisdom. Wisdom was the chief and all-pervading subject of study in the Lord's school. And Daniel is presented to us as a sample of what such teaching will produce. Let such teaching pervade again the Lord's schools, and Daniels will be again produced.

Chapter 11.

The Study of Knowledge.

THE second feature of the education of Daniel and his three companions, and a feature of the instruction in the Lord's schools, is *knowledge*. Those youth were "cunning in knowledge."

As we have seen, the word translated "knowledge" implies information acquired by thinking and application, by study, inquiry, and search. This is the thought of the other scriptures also: "If thou criest after knowledge, and liftest up thy voice for understanding; if thou seekest her as silver, and searchest for her as for hid treasures; then shalt thou understand the fear of the Lord, and find the knowledge of God." Prov. 2:3–5. As we have also seen, knowledge is the complement of wisdom; and is inseparable from wisdom, which is the fear of the Lord and itself the beginning of knowledge. Accordingly, like wisdom, knowledge is the gift of God; for "out of His mouth cometh knowledge and understanding." Prov 2:6. He "teacheth man knowledge." Ps. 94:10.

And "He that teacheth man knowledge, shall not He know?" This is a question propounded by Inspiration itself: and in such a connection that there can be no other reply than that He is the very Fountain of knowledge.

First the question is put (Ps. 94:9), "He that planted the ear, shall He not hear?" The ear is a wonderful instrument, adapted to sound. In the making of the ear, the science of sound was considered, and the instrument was adapted to the science. And before that instrument of hearing was made, He who made its wonderful adaptations *knew what it is to hear*. Next the question is, "He that formed the eye, shall He not see?" The eye is a wonderful instrument, adapted to the light. In the making of the eye, the science of light was considered, and the instrument was adapted to the science. And before there was made that instrument of seeing, He who made it *knew what it is to see*. And finally the question is, "He that teacheth man knowledge, shall not He know?" The mind of man is wonderful creation, adapted to knowledge. In the making of the mind, the whole field and science of knowing were considered, and the mind was adapted to the science and the field. And before there was made that wonderful faculty of knowing, He who made it *knew what it is to know*. *In Him alone*, therefore, is the Fountain of knowledge. From Him alone can come true knowledge; from Him alone can come the science of knowing.

This at once reveals Him as the only true Teacher of man. And this is precisely the attitude in which He presents Himself: "I am the Lord thy God which teacheth thee to profit." Isa. 48:17. "He that is perfect in knowledge is with thee;" and "who teacheth like Him?" Job 36:4, 22.

And "He teacheth man knowledge." That which He teaches is only knowledge: it is that which can be known, not mere theory. It is not mere hypothesis, guess, or conjecture; it is the certitude of knowledge. And He does this as He does all other things—by His Word: for "out of His mouth cometh knowledge." In a previous chapter we have seen that it is only *the truth* that can be known; and that therefore truth is the first essential to knowledge. Now the Word of God *because it is the Word of God* is essential, original, ultimate truth. That Word is therefore the open and sure way to certitude of knowledge.

This thought brings us to the consideration of another very important sense in which the fear of the Lord is the

The Study of Knowledge.

beginning of knowledge, and which illustrates how certainly wisdom and knowledge are inseparable. Unless a person knows a thing *right*, he is not certain of his knowledge nor of himself in it. Certitude is essential to genuine knowledge. "Knowledge" that is derived from guesses is not true knowledge; it is but a guess. For all that can ever be derived from a guess is a guess. "Knowledge" that is gathered from a "working hypothesis" is not genuine knowledge: it is not certainty. All that can ever be evolved from an hypothesis, "working" or other, is an hypothesis. And even though upon the theory of probabilities the conclusion derived from an hypothesis may be considered as established to "a high degree of probability;" yet its essential nature is that of "*probability*" only, and not absolute certainty. With all such "knowledge" there goes a "painful uncertainty" and also the consciousness of it, which of itself vitiates every essential quality of it as being real knowledge.

On the other hand, he who in the fear of God begins with the truth of God for his basis, by this very means begins with the certainty of knowledge. Beginning thus with the certainty of knowledge because he begins with the certainty of truth, and, under the guidance of the Spirit of God who is the Spirit of Truth, following on to know only the truth, the student advances not hesitatingly because of uncertainty, but firmly and certainly because of the certitude of knowledge acquired. As the Word and the works of God are thus studied, "the Holy Spirit flashes conviction into the mind. It is not the conviction which logical reasoning produces; but, unless the mind has become too dark to know God, the eye too dim to see Him, the ear too dull to hear His voice, *a deeper meaning is grasped.*"

It is true that this is not the usual way of seeking knowledge; but it is the right way. The world's way is to begin with "a supposition, a guess, a conjecture," as a basis. But is it not infinitely better, is it not infinitely more sensible, to begin with the certainty of truth, than to begin with a guess? And is not the *truth* of *God* a surer basis than is the *guess* of a *man*?

It is in the nature of things that the mind of man must have a foundation upon which to build, a basis from which to proceed, a premise from which to reason. In this there is universal agreement. The point at which arises the difference between Christianity and the world is, What shall be this foundation, this basis, this premise? and who shall supply it? Shall it be certainty? or shall it be a guess? Shall it be the certainty of the truth of God? or shall it be the uncertainty of the guess of a man? Shall it be supplied by God? or shall it be supplied by man? Shall it be derived from the true and pure Fountain of knowledge? or———?!

Chapter 12.

The Study of Science.

THE third feature of Daniel's education is that he *understood science*. This was but the complement of the second, as the second was the complement of the first. Wisdom, knowledge, and science were these three. Wisdom is the fear of the Lord; this is the beginning of knowledge. Daniel was "skillful in all wisdom;" he was skillful in the fear of the Lord. This being the beginning of knowledge, Daniel had proceeded from this beginning to its complement,—he had observed facts and studied things, and so had become "cunning in knowledge;" and from this, in turn, he had proceeded to *its* complement, and had classified and systematized his knowledge, and so understood science.

This is the divine order in education: first, the fear of the Lord; secondly, knowledge; thirdly, science. First, *the fear of the Lord* as the beginning and the basis of all knowledge; secondly, *knowledge*, acquired from the careful observation of facts and the diligent study of things, in the light and from the basis of the certainty of truth; and thirdly, *science*, as the result of this knowledge classified and systematized.

But where did Daniel or his teachers find any formulated science or any guide to science which might be used as a study in school or as a material part of general education?—Without hesitation it can be said, and truly said, that all this had been matter of common knowledge in Israel for hundreds of years, and at least the principles of it were found in the Holy Scriptures, the Bible of that time.

The Place of the Bible in Education

Solomon lived and taught four hundred years before Daniel's school days. Solomon "was wiser than all men." And what Solomon knew was not kept to himself, locked up in his own understanding; but he taught it to the people. He taught it, too, to all the people; he popularized it. It was so plain and simple that the common people could understand it.

Solomon thoroughly understood what is now called botany, and zoology, and ornithology, and entomology, and ichthyology, and meteorology. For "he spake of trees, from the cedar tree that is in Lebanon even unto the hyssop that springeth out of the wall;" and that is called "botany." "He spake also of beasts;" and that is called "zoology." He spake also "of fowl;" and that is called "ornithology." He spake "of creeping things;" and that is called "entomology." He spake "of fishes;" and that is called "ichthyology." He spake of the course of the wind in "his circuits," of the clouds and the rain: and that is "meteorology." Solomon knew more of *all* these sciences than any man today knows of any *one* of them. And he *taught* them to all the people; for "he spake" of them all. 1 Kings 4:33 Eccl. 1:6, 7; 11:3, 4.

We do not say that Solomon taught "botany" as such, not "zoology" as such, nor "ornithology," nor "entomology," nor "ichthyology," nor "meteorology." We do not say that he taught "science" at all, as it is taught to–day, nor as it is suggested in these big words; that is, science in the abstract. He did not speak of "botany;" he "spake of *trees, from the cedar tree that is in Lebanon even unto the hyssop that springeth out of the wall.*" He did not speak of "zoology;" "he spake of *beasts.*" He did not speak of ornithology;" he spake of *fowl.* He did not speak "entomology;" he spake of "*creeping* things." He did not speak of "ichthyology;" he spake "of *fishes.*" He did not speak of "meteorology;" he spake of the wind in "his circuits," and

The Study of Science.

the returning of "all the rivers" from the sea to the place whence they came to "run into the sea."

That is, he did not give learned and high-sounding discourses on these *subjects*; he spake of the *things* themselves. The very flowers themselves were studied, and discoursed upon; not the flower plucked off, and torn to pieces, and each piece designated by an almost unpronounceable term, and that perhaps in a foreign language,—not this, but the flowers *as they grew*, in garden, field, or forest, just as God caused them to grow, clothed with living beauty. And the lesson which God teaches by each flower was learned from the flower as it stood: for instance, the lovely little violet growing demurely among the grasses. Likewise also the beasts, the birds, the creeping things, and the fishes were studied and discoursed upon *as they were*, alive and before his eyes and the eyes of those to whom "he spake." For Solomon acquired his learning by giving his "heart to seek and to search out *by wisdom* concerning all things that are done under heaven." And as he learned, so he taught.

Such is the way in which science was taught and learned in Israel, where the fear of the Lord was the beginning of all knowledge, the guide in all study, and the basis of all science. It was the study of *things*, rather than a study *about* things. And that is just the difference today that there is between the right and the wrong way of studying science. The right way is to study *things*; the wrong way is to study *about* things. By studying this right way, the student learns always *something*; whereas, by studying the wrong way, he learns only *about* something. The right way gives him practical knowledge; the wrong way gives him but abstract theories, which he has not the gumption to reduce to practise.

Now this genuine science which was taught by Solomon remained with the nation after Solomon had died. Much

The Place of the Bible in Education

of it was written out, and so was accessible to both teachers and students. And above all, the lessons were ever before them in the beasts and the birds, the creeping things and the fishes, in the trees and the flowers, in sky and sea, in the sunshine and the rain, in the wind and the cloud.

We know that it is commonly supposed that "the Jews did not understand science;" that it was only the heathen that had attained to that. The fallacy of such a view is clearly seen by the fact that although at the time when Daniel was carried away captive, Babylon is supposed by these same persons to have stood at the head of the world in scientific attainments, yet when these four young Jews were examined there after three years of study, "in all matters of wisdom and understanding, that the king inquired of them, he found them *ten times* better than all the magicians and astrologers that were in all his realm." Dan. 1:20. These magicians, astrologers, etc., were the scientists of Babylon. Some of them had been the teachers in the school of Babylon, where Daniel was obliged to go and study. Yet when examination day came, Daniel and his companions proved to be *ten times* better informed than all of them. No man in this world could ever teach ten times more than he knew. Therefore it is certain that Daniel and his brethren did not obtain from those teachers their great knowledge. They obtained it from their own Scriptures, under the teaching of the Spirit of God. In other words, they continued in Babylon the same system of study that they had formerly used in the college in Jerusalem; and, in all that was really knowledge in the Babylonian studies, this gave them ten times the advantage of even their teachers there.

Another illustration of the worse than fallacy of this supposition that the Jews did not understand science, while the heathen did, is the fact that in the books today, and in standard school-books, too, it is printed and taught that Anaximander, a Greek, invented the sun-dial about

The Study of Science.

550 B. C., while the sundial was in use in Jerusalem in the reign of Ahaz, nearly *two hundred* years before that. Isa. 38:8; 2 Kings 20:11; 16:1. It is possible that to the belated Greeks, Anaximander's sun-dial was a new invention altogether, and " a great scientific discovery;" but for our part, we refuse to believe the books which teach that the sun-dial was invented by Anaximander or anybody else two hundred years after it was in common use by the Jews in Jerusalem. The truth is that among the Jews only, was known the purest and truest science that was known in the world down at least to the time of Daniel. And when there shall be found again schools that will teach science as it was taught in the school where Daniel learned, there will be found again Daniels in science—even young men who will know ten times as much as even the teachers in schools where the fear of the Lord is not counted as having any connection with science.

No greater mistake has ever been made, no greater loss has ever been incurred, neither by the church nor by the world—and it has been made by both—than the mistake that has been made in separating *the fear of the Lord*—religion—from *science*.

The church, when she ruled the world, held that the fear of the Lord was a matter altogether apart, and had no relation to the observation of facts and the study of things; and so, that religion had nothing to do with science. Consequently, the most "pious" ones, the "saints," turned away from facts and things, shut themselves up in cloisters and cells, or set themselves on the tops of pillars, gave themselves up to "divine meditation," and spent their time in "worshiping" by trying how many times they could bow or prostrate themselves in an hour; or else in drawing finespun distinctions in doctrine, and expounding hair-splitting theories in theology, and then arraigning and hunting as "heretics" all who would not espouse their particular distinction when they themselves could not clearly state it. Then as the number of theological distinctions was increased, "heresies," of course, multiplied. As heresies multiplied, councils were held to set straight the "heretics." In setting straight the heretics, the councils were obliged authoritatively to interpret the Word of God. Different councils interpreted it differently. Appeals were lodged with the bishop of Rome as the chief bishop of "Christendom." And thus it came about that the bishop of Rome became the oracle through whom alone the Word of God could come rightly interpreted, not only to the church, but even to science. Thus was developed the infallibility of "the church," which was but the infallibility of the bishop of Rome as the chief voice in "the church;" for wherever is lodged the authoritative interpretation of the Word of God, or the claim of it, *there* lies infallibility or the claim of it.

The world, on the other hand, of course held that the fear of the Lord was a matter altogether apart, and had no relation to the observation of facts and the study of things; and so held that religion had "nothing to do with science."

Thus originated the conflict between religion and science. This conflict has always continued on the part of the world. But since the Reformation, there has been an effort on the part of the church to connect religion and science. However, in this effort, "science," *as the world had developed it*, was taken as the standard, and the fear of the Lord—religion—was made to conform to it. But this "science" had been built up without the fear of God, and in many cases in direct antagonism to it. And when this was accepted by the church as the standard to which the fear of the Lord must conform, and by which the fear of the Lord must be gauged, this was to make "science," and even science falsely so called, the *beginning* of knowledge, and the fear of the Lord the end; instead of the fear of the Lord being the beginning, and science—true science—the end. Science was made the head, and the fear of the Lord the

The Study of Science.

tail. And thus the Word of God, by which alone the fear of the Lord can be acquired, was made, *even by the church*, subordinate to human, and even antagonistic, "science;" the Word of the Lord must be interpreted by this human and antagonistic "science:" and so infidels and atheists, through this science to which the church deferred, became the oracles through whom alone the Word of God could come rightly interpreted even to the church. And thus is fast developing the infallibility of "science," which, when finished, will be but the infallibility of the dictum of the chief voice in science, speaking *ex cathedra*.

The everlasting truth is that genuine religion and genuine science are inseparable. Neither with Solomon nor with Daniel was there ever any conflict between religion and science. With neither of these was there ever even any variance between religion and science: so that with neither of them was there ever any *accommodation*, any more than any *conflict*, between religion and science. With both of these men, science was what it always is—the complement of religion.

True science is the complement of true religion,— and it is only the complement; it is never the essence. The fear of the Lord is the beginning of knowledge, and it is only the beginning. It is not intended to be anything but the beginning of knowledge. Therefore he who does not take the fear of the Lord, *and use it* for the acquirement of knowledge, makes an infinite mistake. And he who takes the fear of the Lord, and uses it for the acquirement of knowledge, and yet stops short of having his knowledge attain to the grade and character of science, just so far frustrates the real object of his receiving the fear of God to begin with. He who receives that which is the beginning of science, is bound by that very thing, so far as in him lies, to go on and attain the end of that of which he has received the beginning.

The Place of the Bible in Education

And thus with the fear of the Lord as the beginning of science, and science as the inseparable adjunct of the fear of the Lord; with the Word of God as the means of knowing the fear of God, and this same Word as the basis of all science; with the Holy Spirit of God as the great teacher and the only interpreter of the Word of God; true religion and true science will be united, one and inseparable, now and forever: and infallibility will rest where it belongs,—with *God*, the Author of both true religion and true science.

Chapter 13.

The Study of Mental Science.

GOD alone is the Author of true science; and His Word is the only certain foundation of it for man.

All Christian schools must teach science, which is knowledge. Being Christian schools, they are to teach divine science, divine knowledge—not human science. For Jesus, who is the great Teacher in every truly Christian school, "brought into His teaching none of the science of men." "His majesty could not mingle with human science, which will disconnect from the great Source of all wisdom in a day. The topic of human science never escaped His hallowed lips."

In every field of thought or instruction there is a divine science, and there is a human science. And these are contrary the one to the other, because the constant tendency of human science is to separate from the Source of true wisdom. Indeed, the very nature of human science—which, bear in mind, is but human knowledge—is enmity against God.

There are three great root-sciences,—mental science, moral science, and physical science. All conceivable phases of science are but branches of these. And these three are so closely related that neither is, nor can be, complete without the others.

The first of all the sciences, in importance, and indeed in nature, is mental science. First, therefore, in every

The Place of the Bible in Education

system of teaching comes naturally the teaching of mental science.

Mental science, or psychology, if any would rather deal with it as an "ology," is the science of the *mind*. And as it is the *mind* with which every conscious or intelligent thing is done, in the nature of things the knowledge and training of the mind lie first in all teaching.

Again: the only true object of education "is to restore the image of God in the soul." And it is with the mind that we serve the law of God. No greater gift can possibly be bestowed upon any soul than the service of the law of God. No higher nor more honorable position can ever be attained by any creature than to serve the law of God; that is, to be, in his whole being, so completely in harmony with God that every thought, every motive, and every action will be the perfect reflection of the will of God. And "with the mind" this service is accomplished. The mind is the root from which all else in the individual springs: the mind is the pivot, upon which all else turns. This being so, it is certain that, in the very nature of things in the existence of the individual, in all education the knowledge of the mind is first in importance.

As "mental" is mind, mental science is *mind* science, or science of the mind. And as "science" is knowledge, *science* of the mind is *knowledge* of the mind.

How then shall true knowledge of the mind be gained? Investigation of every other subject is made with the mind; knowledge of every other science is gained with the mind. Through the microscope the mind can study and know the most intricate complications, the most infinitesimal bodies, and the most subtle manifestations, in the natural world. Through the telescope the mind can study the planets in almost infinite distances, and learn their characteristics. Thus by these and other like means the mind can explore the whole realm of nature. But how shall the mind

The Study of Mental Science.

investigate the mind? How shall the mind explore the realm of the mind? Can the mind itself do all this concerning itself? Can the mind take a position back of itself, and put itself under a mental microscope composed of itself, and thus itself, through itself, investigate itself? Such a thing is not only mentally but physically impossible.

With the mind we investigate all other things. But in order to investigate and to know the mind itself we must have *another mind*, as really as in order to investigate and to know anything else we must have the mind itself. The individual mind can not take a position back of itself, and examine and analyze itself; but the individual mind *can* find back of itself another Mind, by which true and certain knowledge of the individual mind can be attained. That Mind is the original and ultimate Mind; and so the Source of all knowledge and all true science of mind. Whosoever would find certain knowledge, the true science of the mind, let him ask of Him who is the Source of mind. When we find what God has said of the mind, in that we find the true knowledge of the mind.

He has said that He made man in His own image. Man was made to represent, to reflect, to manifest God—not himself. God made the mind of man that each faculty should be the faculty of the divine Mind: should be the highest created means of expressing, of re-presenting the divine Mind.

All created things are but the expression of the thought of God; for "By the word of the Lord were the heavens made; and all the host of them by the breath of His mouth." "For *He spake*, and it was." By the Word of God "were all things created, that are in heaven, and that are in earth, visible and invisible." Word is the expression of thought, and thought is the product of mind. All created things being the product of the word of God, are only so many forms of expression of the thought of God. The creation of man—the making of mind—was the crowning of creation; therefore the mind of man is the highest created means of reflecting, of re-presenting, of expressing, the thought of God.

Note the divinely-given illustration of this: When God had made the man alone, He caused to pass before him all the beasts and the fowls, "to see what he would call them." *Not*, as many misread it, to have him give names to them; but in truth "to see what he would call them." It was a test of the mind of the man. All these created things, being the product of the word of God, were variant expressions of the thought of God. As each passed before the man, instantly his intellect pierced to the very core of its being, his mind read the thought of God therein expressed, and that thought he reproduced in speaking the word that defined the essential nature and characteristic of each. For "whatsoever Adam called every living creature, that was the name thereof." Whatsoever he called it, that was precisely what it is. This demonstrates that the mind of man was of such breadth that it compassed creation; that it was of such perfect versatility that it readily grasped the characteristics of the vastly varied creation; that it easily moved with such absolute precision as instantly to detect the essential and distinctive nature of each created thing, however subtle that distinction might be; and that his own personality in his own free will was so perfectly submitted to the divine Will, was so perfectly in harmony with the divine Mind, that the thought of that Mind, however expressed, was instantly caught by his mind and became his thought, and he thought the thoughts of God.

Yet this was not all. It was not only in the word of God expressed in the visible creation, that the man found and thought the thoughts of God. The word of God came to the man direct. God spoke directly to the man; so that the man communed with God in the thoughts of God directly communicated in the word and by the Spirit of God. This

The Study of Mental Science.

in the highest possible sense made the mind of man the highest created means of reflecting the divine Mind, of expressing the thought of God, of glorifying God. This is the man, this is the mind, as the man was in the creation of God.

But to the man there came another word, the opposite of the word of God, conveying the thought and mind of the one who is opposed to God. The man had the word of God. So long as he received and held that word, and in that the thought and mind of Him whose word it was, he would in that have held the mind of God as his guiding mind. One expression of that word was: "Of the tree of knowledge of good and evil, thou shalt not eat of it: for in the day that thou eatest thereof thou shalt surely die." This other word that now came to him was: "Ye shall not surely die: for God doth know that in the day ye eat thereof, then your eyes shall be opened, and ye shall become as gods, knowing good and evil." This other word, the opposite of the word of God, was listened to, its thought was received, and in this was received the mind of him whose was the thought and the word. Then with this opposite mind everything was seen in reverse: the tree that was not in any sense good for food, nor to be desired to make one wise, was now seen to be exactly that which it was not. "And when the woman saw that the tree was good for food, and that it was pleasant to the eyes, and a tree to be desired to make one wise, she took of the fruit thereof, and did eat, and gave also unto her husband with her; and he did eat." Thus when Satan came speaking *his* words, conveying the thought and suggestion of his evil mind; and when here was accepted this strange word with its evil thought and suggestion, in place of the word and thought of the mind of God; then the evil mind of the enemy, instead of the mind of God, was received and became the man's guiding mind. That mind being the mind of Satan is enmity against God, for it is not, and can not be, subject to the law of God.

The Place of the Bible in Education

And this is how it is that the mind of man in sin, the natural, "the carnal mind is enmity against God," and "is not subject to the law of God, neither indeed can be."

And now being filled with the evil mind of the enemy, with its perverse desires and bad ambitions, the man reflected the image and shame of him who had led him into sin; instead of as before reflecting the image and glory of Him who had created him in righteousness and true holiness. Just as certainly as *before* man sinned he reflected the image and glory of his Maker unto righteousness, so certainly *after* he sinned he reflected the image and shame of his seducer unto sin.³

The truth of this is seen in every line of the man's conduct immediately after his sinning. The glory had no sooner departed from him because of the sin, than they "were ashamed" before Him in whose presence they had formerly only delighted. *Now* when they heard the voice of God, instead of being filled with joy, they were afraid, and sought to hide from Him, and even thought that they *could* hide, and that they *had hidden*, themselves from Him. Such is not the mind that thinks the thoughts of God. It is instead the very reflection of the mind of Lucifer in heaven, who, not understanding the Lord's purpose, thought that he could hide from the Lord his own purposes.

Again: When the Lord asked the man, "Hast thou eaten of the tree, whereof I commanded thee that thou shoulders not eat?" instead of answering directly and honestly, "I have," he answered indirectly and evasively, and involved in the guilt both the Lord and the woman *before himself*. He said, "The woman *whom Thou gavest* to be with me, *she gave me* of the tree, and *I did eat*." And when the Lord asked the woman, "What is this that thou hast done?"

---

3   Any who desire to follow further this thought of that other mind, can do so by reading Chapter 21 of *Ecclesiastical Empire*.

The Study of Mental Science.

instead of answering plainly and frankly, she also involves another before herself, and shields herself, as had the man. She said, "The serpent beguiled me, and I did eat."

No such mind as that was ever put into mankind by the Lord. Yet everybody knows that this very mind is that which is naturally in all mankind, even to this day. Everybody knows that it is not in the natural man, openly, frankly, and at once, to confess a fault. The spontaneous impulse in every human soul is to dodge and shelter self behind anything or anybody in the world, and seek to clear himself by involving another. And if by all this he can not fully escape, yet when he does come into it, it must be with the least possible degree of blame attaching to himself. Such disposition was never put into mankind by the Lord. It is not of the Lord. It is of Satan. It is the disposition, it is the very mind and spirit, of Lucifer, the original leader in the way of sin.

But the Lord in His love and mercy would not, and did not, leave mankind enslaved and undone through the possession of such a mind. "The Lord God said unto the serpent,...I will put enmity between thee and the woman, and between thy seed and her Seed." By this gracious word, God penetrated and broke up the pall of total darkness that in the mind of Satan had enveloped mankind. By this word He caused the divine light to shine into the darkened mind of the enslaved captive sitting helpless. And this light is "the true Light which enlightens every man on his coming into the world." For this enmity against Satan, this hatred of evil, which God by this word puts into the mind of every person who comes into the world, causes each soul to hate the evil and to desire the good, and to long for deliverance from the bondage of evil into the glorious rest and delight of the good. And as this deliverance is found alone in Christ, that promise to put enmity between Satan and mankind *is the promise of the gift of Christ*, "the Desire of all nations."

The Place of the Bible in Education

This is how it is that "the Son of God is come, and *hath given us a mind*." This is how it is that ever since the hour when that gracious word was spoken to sinful man in the garden, the one first word of God to all mankind is, "Repent:" that is, *change your mind*. Change your mind from the guiding mind of Satan to the guiding mind of God; "Let *this mind* be in *you* which was also in Christ Jesus." This is why it is that men are exhorted by the Word of God, "Be not conformed to this world, but be ye *transformed* by the *renewing of your mind*." And this is why it is and how it is that of all who receive this divine counsel it can be said, "We *have* the *mind of Christ*."

Thus the Ultimate of mind and the Author of the mind of man has spoken on the subject of the mind; and has plainly revealed that there are two minds that are bidding for the choice and study of men. And every man is free to choose which of these two minds he will have to be his guiding mind and the subject of his study in mental science. Which of these two is worthy of the choice of men as the field of mental science?

Of the one mind, the mind of man *as he is*, the natural mind, the Source of mind has said: "The carnal mind is enmity against God." That is the truth from Him who is the Fountain of knowledge. It therefore follows that any human science of the human mind, human psychology, can be only the science of enmity against God; and the study of any human science of the human mind, the study of human psychology, can be only the study of that which is enmity against God.

But what profit is there, what profit can there possibly be, in the study of enmity against God? Suppose that this mind which is enmity against God be studied and analyzed and all its phenomena be marked, *by this mind that is enmity against God*, what will the student have by it all?—Only enmity against God. What does he know?—Only enmity

The Study of Mental Science.

against God. And even this he does not *know*; he *thinks* that it is something else. If he really knew that it is enmity against God, surely he would not study it at all. Surely, then, in no Christian school will any human science of the mind be studied. To know what that is, to know that it is enmity against God, is surely enough to know, without wasting time in any detailed study of it.

Of the other mind, the mind of man *as he was*, the original and spiritual mind, the Source of mind has said that it is "the mind of Christ," who is "God manifest," in whom "dwelleth all the fulness of the God-head bodily," and who is "God." He has said that it is the mind of Him who is "merciful and gracious, long-suffering, and abundant in goodness and truth, keeping mercy for thousands, forgiving iniquity and transgression and sin:" that it is the mind of Him who in a word is "Love;" and who is the Fountain of wisdom and knowledge—of philosophy and science.

Here is a mind that is supremely worthy of the most devoted application in the most profound study. Here is a mind the knowledge of which is only a continual inspiration and an eternal blessing. It is the divine Mind itself. The knowledge of this Mind is in the nature of things divine knowledge. And this knowledge is freely open to us. Yea, this very Mind itself is freely given to us. For He has freely given to us His own eternal Spirit; and it is one of the offices of this eternal Spirit to make known to us the things of God, to take the things of God and show them to us, to fathom the infinite depths of the eternal purpose of God, and to bring forth the treasures of the love, the wisdom, and the knowledge of God and make them plain to our minds and seal them upon our understanding. Therefore the divine exhortation, "Be ye transformed by the renewing of your mind, that ye may prove what is that good, and acceptable, and perfect, will of God." This transformation of life and character, of body, soul, and spirit, through the *renewing of the mind* by faith in Jesus Christ,—this is a mental science, this is a psychology, that is a true science, and worthy of the most industrious and intense application of the powers of teachers and students. And this science is divine. There is, therefore, a divine science of the mind,—a divine psychology open to all the teachers and students in all schools. Shall not, then, this divine mental science be studied in all Christian schools?

Knowledge of the mind must consist of a knowledge of the characteristics, operations, and phenomena of the mind.

Human science of the mind would consist of a systematized knowledge of the characteristics, operations, and phenomena of the human mind.

Divine science of the mind would consist of a systematized knowledge of the characteristics, operations, and phenomena of the divine mind.

Now which of these fields of mental science—the human or the divine presents the fairest prospect for profitable study?

With anybody who believes that there is a divine Mind, and that it is in anywise accessible to the investigation of man, can there be any possible ground of comparison between the human and the divine as a field of profitable study?

Is it not perfectly plain that as certainly as there is a divine Mind, and that that Mind is in any way accessible to investigation by man, so certainly the science of that Mind presents a field as much more promising than does the human, as the divine is above the human?

When one who believes that there is a divine Mind, and that it is accessible to investigation by man, makes the human mind the field of his study in mental science, he thereby puts the human in the place of the divine, places it practically above the divine, and so shows that his

The Study of Mental Science.

professed belief in the divine is but a mere assent, having no weight, and being without effect, in his life.

"But, beloved, we are persuaded better things of you." Heb. 6:9. There is a divine Mind. This divine Mind is open to the study of man. Man is invited and welcomed to investigate the nature and operations of this divine Mind.

The operations of mind, whether divine or human, are solely through thought. And, primarily, thought is expressed in word. The divine thought is expressed in the divine Word. And in the expression of the divine thought, as in no other, words are indeed things. For "in the beginning was the Word" (John 1:1), and "the worlds were framed by the word of God" (Heb. 11:3); "for He spake, and it was." Ps. 33:9.

It was by the word of the Lord that all things were made that are. And as word is the expression of thought, it is plain that all things that are, are but the different forms of the expression of the thought of God. Even so says the Scripture: "Thou, Lord, hast made me glad through Thy work; I will triumph in the works of Thy hands. O Lord, how *great* are Thy *works!* and *Thy thoughts* are *very deep*." Ps. 92:4, 5.

It therefore follows that the proper method of the study of all things that are, is to study them as expressions of the thought of God, and to discover what the thought is that is so expressed. This is but the study, obtaining the knowledge, of the divine Mind; and this, in itself, is divine mental science. Thus all creation is a field of mental science; and all nature-study, properly understood, is the study of the science of the divine Mind.

Reading the thoughts of God, studying the phenomena of the divine Mind, in this vast and wonderful field, is the first occupation in which the newly-created, perfect, and upright man was ever engaged. To this occupation that man was distinctly called and appointed by the Creator

The Place of the Bible in Education

Himself. And though there was more than this one thing in that event, this one thing is in itself divine instruction to all mankind that the first of all occupation that is becoming to man is, under the conscious and recognized divine guidance, the reading of the thoughts and the studying of the phenomena of the mind of God in His wonderful field of creation.

Yet this field of all creation, wonderful as it is, is not all of this great field of mental science. There is another, even more wonderful: "The Lord *thinketh* upon *me*." Ps. 40:17. And, "I know the thoughts that I think toward you, saith the Lord, thoughts of peace, and not of evil." Jer. 29:11. These thoughts are His thoughts of salvation to sinners, the redemption of the lost, and are expressed in the *Word* of His salvation, the gospel of the Lord Jesus Christ. For this gospel is the revelation of "the eternal purpose which He purposed in Christ Jesus our Lord."

These two great realms of mental science—the thoughts of God in creation and the thoughts of God in redemption—were the fields of study of Solomon, the wisest man who ever lived since Adam. But now, since man has become subject to sin, the field of the thought of God in redemption takes precedence; because man must be saved from the darkness and perversion of mind into which he was seduced by Satan, before he can correctly read the thoughts of God expressed in creation. Accordingly, though Solomon gave his heart to seek and to search out all things that are done under heaven, and was supremely successful in this, yet it was "by wisdom," which is "the fear of the Lord," that he did it. Accordingly also he exalts wisdom, the fear of the Lord, as the one chief thing of all things to be desired. Prov. 3:15.

For this reason, with Christ also, the one model Man of all the ages, and the last Adam, the thought of God in redemption was the field of transcendent importance for

The Study of Mental Science.

the occupation of the mind of man: not by any means to the exclusion of the field of creation, but because of its being the only true way into the light in which the thought of God in creation can be clearly seen and correctly read.

Nor is it alone to men on the earth and in sin that the thought of God in the field of redemption, the gospel of Christ, is held to be of transcendent importance in understanding the depth of meaning in the other realm of God's thought. It reaches even to unfallen worlds and to the bright intelligences of heaven itself. The thoughts of God, involved in His eternal purpose, and expressed in His Word of the gospel, are the chief science of the heavenly intelligences. For the preaching of "the unsearchable riches of Christ" is to "make all see what is the fellowship of the mystery, which from the beginning of the world hath been hid in God, who created all things by Jesus Christ; *to the intent* that *now* unto *the principalities and powers* in *heavenly places* might be known by [through, by means of] the church the manifold wisdom of God, according to the eternal purpose which He purposed in Christ Jesus our Lord." Eph. 3:8–11.

And when this is preached "with the Holy Ghost sent down from heaven," "the angels *desire*," with intense interest, "to *look into*" it, that they may behold the manifold wisdom revealed in the operation of the divine Mind in working out that eternal purpose 1 Peter 1:12.

Here, then, are two infinite realms of the science of the divine Mind, opened to the investigation of man. And both center in Jesus Christ; for in both, all the phenomena are the expressions of the thought of the divine Mind; and as *thought* is expressed in *word*, and Jesus Christ is the *Word* of God, so, whether in creation or in redemption, Jesus Christ, being the *Word* of God, is the expression of the *thought* of God. And as Jesus Christ is the expression of the thought of God in these two wonderful fields of the operation of the divine Mind, it is perfectly plain that without Him the thoughts expressed in these fields can not be understood.

In view of these things, is it not perfectly plain, and easily understood, why "Jesus brought into His teaching none of the science of men"? why "His majesty could not mingle with human science"? why "the topic of human science never escaped His hallowed lips"? and why it is that "human science will disconnect from the great Source of all wisdom in a day"?

And when men leave this wonderful double field of the science of the divine Mind, and spend their time and effort in the dark and narrow field of the operation of the human mind, which is enmity against God, is it not true that they have left the beautiful waters of the snow of Lebanon, which come from the Rock of the field, for "the murky waters of the valley"? yea, that they have turned even to "common sewers"? And when that is done, can there be any wonder that "the result" is "parched hearts in the school and in the church"?

Shall not Christian schools, then, teach as mental science only the science of the divine Mind?

Chapter 14.

The Study of Moral Science.

MORAL science must be taught in every Christian school. This is no less important than the teaching of mental science, though in the nature of things it is second in *order* to mental science, because it is only with the *mind* that it can be studied.

Right *morals* can be discerned only with a right *mind*. Therefore true moral science can be understood only through true mental science. Thus, though in this sense moral science is second in *order* to mental science, it is not less in importance; indeed, the two are inseparably connected.

However, though we speak of these as "moral science" and "mental science," and treat them as sciences which they truly are, let no one fall into the mistake of thinking that these sciences are abstruse things, obscured and confused under long sentences of high-sounding words, and beyond the reach of people of common understanding. It is not so. True science is always simple and easily understood. The nearer true, and the better understood, any science is, the simpler it is, and the plainer it can be made to those who would know it.

"Morals" is the common name for *virtue*: so that moral science, or the science of morals, is the science of virtue. And virtue pertains to right, the good, the true, the pure. It relates to *conduct*, and conduct relates to character. In other words, moral science is *character*-science. And science is knowledge. Fully expressed in other words, then, as

The Place of the Bible in Education

morals is *character*, and *science* is *knowledge*, moral science is *character-knowledge;* the *science of morals* is the *knowledge of character.*

What shall be the field, then, for the study of moral science? What *character* shall be the basis and subject of this *knowledge?* Shall it be the human character, or the divine character? That is to say, Shall it be human moral science, or shall it be divine moral science, that shall be studied in Christian schools?

As these schools profess to be Christian, the only moral science that can there be consistently studied is *Christian* moral science. Christian character is the character of Jesus Christ, and the character of Christ is the character of God; therefore, the only character-science that can be consistently studied in any Christian school is science of the character of God.

In education, character is everything. In all true education the one chief aim, the one thing to which all other things must tend and must be made to contribute, is *character.* For it is even written that, though I have understanding of the profoundest philosophy, and of all science; and though I have such versatility and eloquence that in these I could speak with the tongues of men and of angels; yet "I am *nothing*" if I have not charity, which is simply supreme character, "the bond of perfectness." And we have seen in Greece and Rome the vicious nature and ruinous results of the highest classical education without character: of the almost perfect mental and physical culture without morals.

The story of man's morals is parallel to the story of man's mind. This is inevitable, for the mind is the citadel of morals: "As he thinketh in his heart, so is he:" "With the mind I serve the law of God."

God made the man upright, in His own image, clothed with His own glory, reflecting His own character. God

The Study of Moral Science.

made the man to stand in this estate forever: yet free to choose not so to stand. And the man did choose not so to stand with God; but to take the way of Satan and sin. Instead of abiding forever in the realm of God and His righteousness, the man chose the realm of Satan and his sin, the realm of the transgression of the law of God, the realm of immorality.

If it be asked. Could not God have made the man so that he could not sin? the perfectly safe and true answer is, *He could not*. That is. He could not so make him *a man*: so to have made him would have been to make him unintelligent, a mere animal machine, incapable of morals. For to have made the man so that he simply *could* not sin, would have been equally to make him so that he could not do right. It would have been to make him so that he could not choose: and to have made him unable to choose would have been to make him incapable of virtue. Freedom of choice is essential to morals. God made man to be moral. Therefore He made him free to choose. And He forever respects that of which He is the Author, the freedom of choice in man. He Himself will never invade a hair's breadth the freedom of man to choose for himself.

Thus in His wisdom God created the man upright, holy, and free, only "a little lower than the angels." He gave to him paradise for his home. He gave to him dominion over the earth and over every living thing upon it, as the representative of God. He made to grow from the ground "every tree that is pleasant to the sight, and good for food," and "the tree of life, which is in the midst of the paradise of God." He gave to him everything that could please the eye, charm the senses, and delight the mind. He gave it all to the holy pair to be enjoyed by them forever. He made them free to enjoy it or to refuse it: therefore He put also in the midst of the garden the *forbidden* tree, "the tree of knowledge of good and evil." "And the Lord God commanded the man, saying, Of every tree of the garden thou mayest freely eat; but of the tree of the knowledge of good and evil, thou shalt not eat of it; for in the day that thou eatest thereof thou shalt surely die." Thus for the man then, as for man forever, there was established the principle, "Choose you this day whom ye will serve:" the divine principle of self-government, and government with the consent of the governed.

And in the exercise of the freedom of choice the man chose not to govern himself, but to sell himself to Satan in the bondage of sin and to the principle of lawlessness—immorality. And just there when the man had sinned and was lost, Christ offered Himself to save him. And the only reason why the man did not die that day, even in the very hour in which he sinned, is that *just then* Jesus Christ offered Himself in his behalf, and took upon Himself the death that would have then fallen upon the man; and thus gave to man another chance, a probation, a breathing space, that he might choose life. This is how God could immediately say to the deceiver: "I will put enmity between thee and the woman, and between thy seed and her Seed." This is how it is that He is "the Lamb slain from the foundation of the world;" and how He can say forever, "I am come that *they might have life*, and that they might have it more abundantly."

Here it may be queried: As God made man, and of course all intelligent creatures, free to choose, and therefore free to choose the way of sin if they should so choose, did He not then have to provide against this possible choice, *before* man was made?—The answer is, Certainly He did. And since He made and must make all creatures of moral sense also thus free to choose, He had to make provision for the possibility of the entrance of sin, even before ever there was a single intelligent creature created. And *He did so*. This provision is but a part of that eternal purpose which He purposed in Christ Jesus our Lord.

The Study of Moral Science.

Let us, in thought, go back to when there was no created person or thing: back to the eternal counsels of the Godhead. The existence of God is not a self-satisfied existence. His love is not self-love. His joy is not fulfilled in wrapping Himself within Himself, and so sitting solitary and self-centered. His love is satisfied only in flowing out to those who will receive and enjoy it to the full. His joy is fulfilled only in carrying to an infinite universe, full of blessed intelligences, the very fulness of joy.

Standing, then, in thought, with God before there was a single intelligent creature, He desires that the universe shall be full of joyful intelligences enjoying His love to the full. In order that this shall be, they must all choose to enjoy His love and His joy. In order to choose this, they must be *free* to choose it. And in order to be free to choose it, they must be free *not* to choose it: free to choose not to serve Him, to choose not to enjoy His love and joy. They must be free to choose Him or themselves, life or death. This involves the possibility that some will choose not His way, but their own way apart from Him; and so involves the possibility of the entrance of selfishness, the entrance of sin, which is directly the opposite of all that is Himself. Shall He then refuse to create intelligences at all because if He creates, it must be with the possibility that sin may enter? If this shall be the decision, the result could only be that He must eternally remain self-centered and solitary. But that itself is also the opposite of all that is Himself. Therefore to decide thus would be to decide that He would cease to be God. But He can not cease to be God; "He can not deny Himself;" therefore He must create even to the infinite limit.

And He did create. He created intelligences. He created them free to choose: free to choose His way, or to choose the opposite: and therefore free to sin *if* they choose. And *at the same time*, in His infinite love and eternal righteousness, He *purposed* to give Himself in sacrifice to redeem all who would sin; and give to them a *second* freedom to choose Him or themselves, life or death. And those who, against all this, would the second time choose death, let them have what they have persistently chosen. And those who would choose life—the universe full of them—let them enjoy to the full that which they have chosen: even eternal life, the fulness of perfect love and of bliss forevermore.

This is God, the living God, the God of love, the God and Father of our Lord Jesus Christ, who is fully able to do whatsoever He will in heaven and earth, and yet leave all His creatures free. This is He who from the days of eternity "worketh all things after the counsel of His own will." And this is "the mystery of His will,...which He hath purposed in Himself; that in the dispensation of the fulness of times He might gather together in one all things in Christ, both which are in heaven, and which are on earth; even in Him." This is "the eternal purpose which He purposed in Christ Jesus our Lord." in whom God reconciles the world unto Himself.

Yet even in this supreme and divine act of reconciliation, God does not seek to bind man to Himself in an absolute and irresponsible bondage, as Satan bound him when his way was chosen. God ever respects the freedom of choice of which He is the Author. He will not even now compel man to take the way of righteousness, nor compel him to keep that way after he has chosen it. When that creative word was spoken, "I will put enmity" between mankind and the enemy, He made man free again, *to choose for himself* whom he will serve. By that word man's will is freed, and forever abides free, to choose to serve whom he will, to choose deliverance from the bondage of sin or to remain in it.

This word of God which plants in each soul enmity against Satan; this hatred of evil that desires deliverance

The Study of Moral Science.

which is found only in Christ;—this is the gift of faith to man. The object of this faith is Christ, and the Author of it is Christ: and so He is the Author and Finisher of faith. Heb. 12:2. Thus the planting of eternal enmity between Satan and the woman, and between the seed of these, was the beginning of the revelation of the mystery of God which had been "kept in silence through times eternal." Rom. 16:25, R. V. And "when the fulness of the time was come, God sent forth His Son, made of *a woman*, made under the law, to redeem them that were under the law, that we might receive the adoption of sons." Gal. 4:4, 5. Then were seen and heard things which many prophets and righteous men had desired to see and had not seen, and had desired to hear and had not heard. Matt. 13:16, 17. And then in the words of Him who spake as never man spake, there were uttered things which had "been kept secret from the foundation of the world." Matt. 13:35.

Thus Christ in His gospel is the one only Way from sin to righteousness, from vice to virtue, from immorality to morality. "For by grace are ye saved *through faith*; and that not of yourselves: it is the gift of God: not of works, lest any man should boast. For we are *His* workmanship, *created* in Christ Jesus *unto good works* [unto morals], which God hath *before ordained that we should walk in* them." Eph. 2:8–10. And thus moral science stands equally with the thought of redemption in mental science, as preceding the study of the thought of God as expressed in the original or physical creation. The thought, the word, and the work of God in the moral creation, in His creating the lost soul unto the good works—the morals—which He originally ordained as the way of man, must be known and understood, before these can be correctly known or understood in the physical creation. For it is only "through faith" that "we understand" or can understand "that the worlds were framed by the word of God, so that things which are seen were not made of things which do appear." Heb. 11:3.

The Place of the Bible in Education

Therefore, after *wisdom*, which is the fear of the Lord, and the beginning of knowledge, Solomon, the wisest man who ever lived since Adam, exalted *morals* as the sum of all books and of all study, the conclusion of all that has been or can be said: "Fear God, and keep His commandments: for this is the whole duty of man." Eccl. 12:13. And one reason why wisdom stands in the lead of all things, is that she "leads in the way of righteousness," which is morals. Prov. 8:20. And that "One greater than Solomon," the model Man of all the ages, and "the last Adam," also exalts morals to this same place: "Seek ye first the kingdom of God, and His *righteousness*." Matt. 6:33. The righteousness of God is the only true morality. The law of God is the only true moral law. And the Book of God, the teaching, the instruction, of God is the only true moral instruction.

What, then, does this Book, this instruction, of Him who "is perfect in knowledge" say on this subject of morals? What does it say to the morals, the character, of man *as he is*: human morals?—Here is the Word of Him who teacheth man knowledge: "Both Jews and Gentiles...are all under sin; as it is written, There is none righteous, no, not one: there is none that understandeth, there is none that seeketh after God. They are all gone out of the way, they are together become unprofitable; there is none that doeth good, no, not one. Their throat is an open sepulcher; with their tongues they have used deceit; the poison of asps is under their lips: whose mouth is full of cursing and bitterness: their feet are swift to shed blood: destruction and misery are in their ways: and the way of peace have they not known: there is no fear of God before their eyes." Rom. 3:9–18. "Out of the heart of men, proceed evil thoughts, adulteries, fornications, murders, thefts, covetousness, wickedness, deceit, lasciviousness, an evil eye, blasphemy, pride, foolishness: all these evil things come from within, and defile the man." Mark 7:21–23.

The Study of Moral Science.

That is a sketch of human character by the One who certainly knows. And the study of human moral science is simply the study of that sort of character: or rather the study of men's conception of that sort of character. And in this, men's conceptions are altogether amiss; for the writers on moral science do not believe that human character is such as is here truly described. They conceive of it as a far different thing. But when moral science is "the science of human duty, *based on a knowledge of human nature*, its springs and faculties of action;" and when men's conceptions of human nature are altogether different from what human nature really and truly is, and these false conceptions of human nature are built up into a "moral science" for the guidance of men; it is perfectly plain that the whole worldly idea of moral science is not only "science falsely so called," but is a fatal delusion.

Moral science is "the science of human duty, based on *a knowledge of human nature, its springs and faculties of action*, and [a knowledge] of the various relations in which man, as a moral and social being, is, or may be, placed." And it must not be forgotten, in the study of any science, that *a guess* is not *knowledge*, *conjecture* is not knowledge, *hypothesis* is not knowledge; but that knowledge is to *know*, to know for *certain*. It is to know, and to know that we know.

Where, then, shall be found the certainty of "*knowledge* of human nature, its springs and faculties of action," etc.?—Certainly only with Him who is perfect in knowledge, who is indeed the Fountain of knowledge. and who teacheth man knowledge. Only this can possibly be the true knowledge of human nature. And only that which is built on *this* knowledge of human nature can possibly be true moral science.

The true knowledge of human nature *as it i*s, He has revealed to us in the passages of revelation above quoted. But surely no person who believes that revelation, no one who receives as the truth that knowledge of human nature, would ever think for a moment of using it as a basis upon which to build the science of human duty. For that revelation, that true knowledge, of human nature, shows that all that human nature is essentially immorality. And any science of which that is the basis, is clearly immoral, not moral, science: is but the science of immorality. And the study of any such "moral science" is only the study of immorality. Of course it is not meant to be that. By the misconception of what human nature really is, such study is supposed to be the study of veritable morals. But in the light of the true knowledge of what human nature really is, it is as plain as A B C that the study of human moral science is but the study of immorality. This can be tested by any one for himself by reading the books that are published as treatises and text-books on moral science. They will almost invariably be found to be essentially pagan, where they are not essentially papal, which is worse. So entirely is this true, that, with one exception, or possibly two, we have never yet seen, and we do not believe there is in the world, a work on moral science, as such, which is not essentially pagan, where it is not essentially papal. This is because the true. the divine, basis of morals is not discerned: but the human lingers through all. It is the tree of the knowledge of good *and* evil: which in essence and at the last is found to be only *evil*. Yet these books—books in which there is neither true morals nor true science—have been and are used as text-books on moral science in professed Christian schools. This will never do. Christianity is of the tree of life. Prov. 3:18.

It is not the science of human nature *as it is*, but of human nature *as it was* and *as it must be*, that is the true moral science. It is not the knowledge, even the perfect knowledge, of human nature *as it is* with its springs and faculties of action, that is the basis of true moral science: that, as we have seen, could be only the perfect knowledge

The Study of Moral Science.

of immorality. The perfect knowledge of human nature *as it was* and as it must be, with *its* springs and faculties of action—only this can possibly be the basis of true moral science: this is the perfect knowledge of perfect human nature with its perfect springs and faculties of action, and is therefore the perfect knowledge of perfect morals. This knowledge is revealed in Jesus Christ in human nature; and is found in *the Word* of that revelation from the day that human nature departed from what *it was* until the day when human nature shall be fully redeemed to what *it must be*. Human nature *as it is*, is blind, in the darkness, sunken in sin, and under the dominion of Satan. Human nature as *it was* and as *it must be*, sees clearly, is in the light, is freed from sin, and is in the kingdom and under the dominion of God in Christ. "Delivering thee from the people, and from the Gentiles, unto whom now I send thee, to open their eyes, and to turn them from darkness to light, and from the power of Satan unto God, that they may receive forgiveness of sins, and inheritance among them which are sanctified by faith that is in Me." Acts 26:17, 18. Christianity, then, the science of Christianity, as it is in the Book of Christianity—the Word made flesh, the gospel of Christ—is the only true moral science.

What, then, is the true human nature as it was and as it must be?—It is human nature partaking of the divine nature. It is the human and the divine joined in one divine-human Man. This is Christ, the model Man. He being God became man: being Divine became human: being the Word of God and God, "was made flesh, and dwelt among us,...full of grace and truth," "God manifest in the flesh," "God with us." And now human nature that is "far off" from God, is "made nigh by the blood of Christ." "For He is *our peace*, who hath made *both* [God and man, the divine and the human] *one*,...having abolished *in His flesh the enmity*,...for to make in Himself *of twain* [God and man] *one new man*, as making peace." Eph. 2:14, 15. And

The Place of the Bible in Education

thus His divine power has given to all men "exceeding great and precious promises; that *by these* YE might be *partakers of the divine nature,* having escaped the corruption that is in the world through lust." 2 Peter 1:4.

What character is the true character of this true man this man as he was and as he must be? What character can alone be becoming to him?—The divine character, of course: the divine character manifest in human nature. This is Christ; and this is the object of the gospel of Christ forever. Therefore "I am not ashamed of the gospel of Christ:...for *therein* is *the righteousness* [the character] of God revealed" Rom. 1:16, 17. Thus the gospel is ever only "God manifest in the flesh," "God with us," and "Christ in you the hope of glory."

What, then, is this character in itself? What is the certainty of knowledge of this character as the basis of moral science? Here it is: "I will make all My goodness pass before thee, and I will proclaim the name of the Lord before thee....And the Lord passed by before him, and proclaimed, The Lord, The Lord God, merciful and gracious, long-suffering, and abundant in goodness an truth, keeping mercy for thousands, forgiving iniquity and transgression and sin, and before whom no man is guiltless." Ex. 33:19; 34:6,7. "God is love." 1 John 4:8 "God so loved the world, that He gave His only-begotten Son, that whosoever believeth in Him should not perish, but have everlasting life." John 3:16 "I have loved thee with an everlasting love: therefore with loving-kindness have I drawn thee." Jer.31:3.

And "God, who commanded the light to shine out of darkness, hath shined in our hearts, to give the light of the knowledge [the science] of the glory [the character] of God in the fact of Jesus Christ." And "we all, with open fact beholding as in a glass the glory [the character] of the Lord, are changed into the same image from glory to glory

The Study of Moral Science.

[from character to character], even as by the Spirit of the Lord." 2 Cor. 4:6; 3:18.

Here is a character that is entirely worthy of the most devoted contemplation. Here is the very perfection of morals. Knowledge of this character is the trust moral science. And the diligent, earnest, prayerful study of this blessed transformation of the soul, through the faith of Jesus Christ and the power of the Spirit of God, from evil to good, from wickedness to righteousness, from sin to holiness, from the human character to the divine character, from immorality to morality, — the study of this is the study of the true science of morals, and is the only true moral science.

In the realm of morals, which is character, since men have forgotten the true morality, and have become altogether immoral; since "they have all gone out of the way," and have "together become unprofitable;" since "there is none that seeketh after God,"—unless God should abandon them utterly, it is essential that there should be set before men the true standard of character in such a way that they shall be drawn to the contemplation of it.

Yet though man had become altogether immoral, God could not abandon him; because He is "the Lord, the Lord God, merciful and gracious, long-suffering, and abundant in goodness and truth, keeping mercy for thousands, forgiving iniquity and transgression and sin." Therefore He formulated for man a transcript of His own character in such a form as to be particularly adapted to the condition and needs of man altogether *as he is*.

This transcript of the character of God, this true standard of character, is formulated in the Law of God, the ten commandments. And while "the God of nature has written His *existence* in all *His works*," He has also "written *His law* in the *heart of man*." And here is the Law of God:—

The Place of the Bible in Education

"I AM

The Lord Thy God,

which have brought thee out of the land of Egypt, out of the house of bondage.

I.

"Thou shalt have no other gods before Me.

II.

"Thou shalt not make unto thee any graven image, or any likeness of anything that is in heaven above, or that is in the earth beneath, or that is in the water under the earth: thou shalt not bow down thyself to them, nor serve them: for I the Lord thy God am a jealous God, visiting the iniquity of the fathers upon the children unto the third and fourth generation of them that hate Me: and showing mercy unto thousands of them that love Me, and keep My commandments.

III.

"Thou shalt not take the name of the Lord thy God in vain: for the Lord will not hold him guiltless that taketh His name in vain.

IV.

"Remember the Sabbath day, to keep it holy. Six days shalt thou labor, and do all thy work: but the seventh day is the Sabbath of the Lord thy God: in it thou shalt not do any work, thou, nor thy son, nor thy daughter, thy manservant, nor thy maidservant, nor thy cattle, nor thy stranger that is within thy gates: for in six days the Lord made heaven and earth, the sea, and all that in them is, and rested the seventh day: wherefore the Lord blessed the Sabbath day, and hallowed it.

The Study of Moral Science.

V.

"Honor thy father and thy mother: that thy days may be long upon the land which the Lord thy God giveth thee.

VI.

"Thou shalt not kill.

VII.

"Thou shalt not commit adultery.

VIII.

"Thou shalt not steal.

IX.

"Thou shalt not bear false witness against thy neighbor.

X.

"Thou shalt not covet thy neighbor's house, thou shalt not covet thy neighbor's wife, nor his manservant, nor his maidservant, nor his ox, nor his ass, nor anything that is thy neighbor's."

It was necessary for the Lord to present His law, the transcript of His character, *in this form*, just *because* of the essential immorality of mankind. For "the law is not made for a righteous man, but for the lawless and disobedient, for the ungodly and for sinners, for unholy and profane, for murderers of fathers and murderers of mothers, for manslayers, for whoremongers, for them that defile themselves with mankind, for men-stealers, for liars, for perjured persons, and if there be any other thing that is contrary to sound doctrine." 1 Tim. 1.9,10.

As this is a description of man just as he is naturally, in the world, it is easy to see how perfectly adapted to his condition, how perfectly calculated to awaken him and draw him away from himself, is that law of universal and

The Place of the Bible in Education

everlasting "Thou shalt not's" absolutely prohibiting him from doing everything that is naturally in him to do. This reveals to man the true knowledge of himself; that he is altogether wrong, a complete sinner. At the same time there is pressing upon him that divinely implanted enmity against Satan. the hatred of evil and desire for the good; with the fatal consciousness that of himself there is no possibility of attaining to the perfection of conduct demanded by that law and sanctioned by the soul's desire. Thus the soul-conflict is deepened till in desperation he cries, "O wretched man that I am! who shall deliver me from the body of this death?" Then, in answer, "the Desire of all nations" comes, and presents Himself to him; and when accepted by him, delivers him from the bondage of corruption into the glorious liberty of the children of God.

So "the *Law entered*, that the offense might abound. *But where sin* abounded, *grace* did *much more* abound: THAT *as sin hath reigned unto death*; EVEN so might *grace reign* through *righteousness* unto *eternal life* by *Jesus Christ* our Lord." Rom. 5:20,21. And "What Law could not do, in so far our earthly nature weakened its action, *God did*, by sending His own Son, with a nature like our sinful nature, to atone for sin. He doomed sin in that earthly nature, so that the requirements of the Law might be satisfied in our lives, lived now in obedience, not to our earthly nature, but to the Spirit." Rom. 8:3,4.

Accordingly, "we know that everything said in the Law is addressed to those who are under its authority, in order that every mouth may be closed, and the whole world become liable to the judgment of God. For no human being will stand right with God as the result of actions done in obedience to Law; for through Law there comes a clear conception of sin. But now, quite apart from Law, there stands revealed a righteousness [a character] which comes from God, and to which the law and the Prophets bear witness. It is a righteousness [a morality] which comes

The Study of Moral Science.

from God through faith in Jesus Christ, and is for all, without distinction, who believe in Him. For all have sinned [have become immoral], and all fall short of God's glorious ideal, but, in His mercy, are being set right with Him through the deliverance which is in Christ Jesus. For God placed Him before the world, to be, by His sacrifice of Himself, a means of reconciliation through faith in Him. God did this, in order to prove His righteousness [His morality], and because in His forbearance He had passed over the sins men had previously committed: God did this, I repeat, as a proof, at the present time, of His own righteousness, in order that He might be righteous [moral], and make those who have faith in Jesus stand right [moral] with Himself." Rom. 3:19–26.

This is the morally scientific way of human nature from what it is to what it must be. to be truly moral.

Chapter 15.

The Study of Physical Science.

IN the realm of physical science the Bible is not the direct and full *treatise* that it is in the mental and moral sciences. Yet all that is said in the Bible touching any of the physical sciences is as certainly true as is what is therein said on any other subject.

For instance, the Bible said that the atmosphere has "weight" three thousand years before Torricelli discovered and announced it to astonished because benighted Europe. The Bible said that one star differs from another star in brightness and beauty—"in glory"—more than seventeen hundred years before astronomers discovered that it was actually a difference in *glory* instead of in *distance*. The Bible said that there is "healing" in the sun's rays, two thousand two hundred and ninety years before medical science made the discovery of it.[4]

These instances are sufficient for illustration, though many more might be cited. These statements of the Bible were all these ages true—scientifically true. If men had read the Bible with anointed eyes and enlightened minds, and had believed simply what it said, they would have all these ages know these scientific truths. And the men who did believe these Bible statements seventeen hundred to three thousand years ago, knew these scientific truths as

---

[4] Upon the authority of that Scripture text alone, the writer of this book, in public addresses, urged physicians to search for that healing in the sun's rays, before Dr. Finsen made his scientific discovery of his ancient Biblical-scientific truth.

The Place of the Bible in Education

certainly as any scientist or anybody else has known them since their discovery.

When the Bible is studied with enlightened and devout mind, it will very soon be discovered that there is far more therein said touching natural philosophy and physical science than is believed even by the vast majority of Christians. And in all these things speaking the truth in the perfection of knowledge, the Bible is thus the true guide in the study of physical science as well as in the study of the mental and moral sciences. The Bible is therefore altogether worthy to be the text-book in physical science as well as in every other line of study, and should be given that place, in every Christian school. In this book it would be too much to undertake extensively to trace each phase of physical science as touched in the Bible. All that can he here attempted is merely a brief running sketch illustrative of how, and how trustworthily, the Bible can be used as at least the test book in the realm of physical science in Christian schools.

The Bible is the true and perfectly reliable basis of the study of physical science, because it is the true and perfectly reliable record of creation. And *Creation*, not evolution, is the origin of all things. Creation by the Word of God being the origin of all physical as of all spiritual existences under God, Revelation by the Word of God is the true and reliable source of all instruction in physical as well as in spiritual science. As already indicated (p. 117,) true knowledge and understanding of the spiritual creation: "Through *faith* we *understand* that *the worlds* were framed by the Word of God, so that things which are seen were not made of things which do appear." That is well. But far more needed than is that, and far more profitable, to be made far more of, is the reverent recognition and devout study of *spiritual law in the natural world*. Faith, *faith* is the way to knowledge and understanding in the physical as in the spiritual world: for all worlds are of God, by the

The Study of Physical Science.

Word of God; as is faith also of God, by the Word of God. Gen. 1:1; Ps. 33:6, 9; Heb. 11:3; Eph. 2:8; Heb. 12:2; Rom. 10:17.

Many even of professed Christians are quite incredulous of the proposition that for Christians the Bible must be the basis of all true education and the textbook in every line of study. They "can not see how this can be so," because they do not believe it; and then will not believe it, because they can not see it. But the only real ground of this incredulity is the exceedingly small place that the Bible occupies in their lives. That place is so very small, so utterly narrow and confined, that in their estimation, to undertake to make the Bible the basis of all education and the textbook in every line of study, is equivalent to teaching practically nothing at all. It is therefore literally the truth that the attitude which each one occupies toward this proposition publishes the measure that the Bible occupies in that person's life.

However, there is a very common mistake that is made with respect to the use of the Bible as the textbook in all studies. With many the idea obtains that this means that the Bible must be the only *study*-book: the only book used in school. Even if this were so, used by those who know the Bible, it would be far better than is now done in popular education. But that is not by any means what is meant. There is a very material difference between a *text*-book and a *study*-book. This mistake or thinking that the Bible as the *text*-book means the Bible as the only *study*-book came about by the fact that in the schools of the day all study-books are called text-books. To the *teachers* these books are supposed to be *text*-books; while to the students they are expected to be study-books. But instead of the study-books of the students being textbooks to the teachers, nine times out of ten the textbooks are study-books to the teachers; and the teachers do not get out of the text-books, and the students hardly ever get into the study-book.

The Bible is a book of *principles*, that are the sure guide in the right way in everything that pertains to the life. The Bible as the text-book therefore is *not* the Bible merely as a storehouse of worthy sentiments, sayings, or mottoes, from which can be selected a sentence or a verse as the basis of a lecture, or the suggestion of a disquisition. The Bible as the text-book is the Bible as the book of *divine principles* which are the life and guide of study, the light to lighten the path of the student, that *the truth*, and only the truth, in philosophy and science, shall be known. The use of the Bible as the text-book of all study is to know in the Bible the *principle*, to plant yourself upon that principle as your firm basis and sure guide, and then from this basis and in the light of this principle use all the realm of nature, revelation, and human experience as the *study*-book.

Chapter 16.

The Study of Physical Science—Anatomy.

OF all the subjects in the realm of physical science, that which most concerns man, that which enters most fully and vitally into his own life, is the science of his own body: the knowledge of its construction, of its preservation, and of its functions. This is true also from the fact that man himself is the crown of creation; and from the further fact that of him Inspiration has declared that he is "fearfully and wonderfully made."

As a perfect illustration of the principle of the Bible as the text-book in science, and of the teaching and science that is truly Christian, the author is permitted to present an address on "How to Study Anatomy," by Stephen Smith, M. D. LL. D., of New York City, which was delivered to the students of the Medical Department of the Syracuse University, Oct. 13, 1902. and published in the *Medical Record.* Jan. 3, 1903.[5]

HOW TO STUDY ANATOMY

"An accurate and practical knowledge of the mechanism of the human body lies at the foundation of true success in the pursuit of the profession of medicine. It is of

---

[5] This address is here printed with the special permission of Dr. Smith and the editor of the *Medical Record*. It is a splendid illustration not only of the use of the Bible as the text-book in science, but of the idea of this whole book. For this reason, the author gratefully acknowledges the great favor in the permission to embody it in his book.

The Place of the Bible in Education

the utmost importance, therefore, that you should at the outset adopt a plan of study which, while it fascinates, and thus absorbs all your attention, tends also powerfully to fix firmly in your memory the associated relations of function and structure. It is only when these relations are so thoroughly grasped and retained by the mind that structure at once suggests function, and function suggests structure, that anatomy is made available in all the emergencies of the daily practise of medicine and surgery.

"It can not be denied that the present method of studying anatomy does not, as a rule, accomplish this result. How rarely does a student become so interested in the study of anatomy that in his zeal in its pursuit he neglects his other studies, or sacrifices pleasures and amusements! And, what is more important, how seldom do we meet a practitioner who can readily recall the precise anatomy and functions of even the more important organs and structures of the body! If we examine critically the modern text-books on anatomy, for the purpose of determining their adaptation to the twofold purpose of inspiring the student with a genuine love of the science and of rendering his knowledge instantly available in practise, we shall be convinced that they accomplish neither result; nor is it difficult to explain the cause of failure. The course of study is entirely wanting in that system, or orderly and logical development of the structures of the body, which appeals to the inventive and constructive faculties. Instead of being treated as an entity, in which each organ and structure contributes in due proportion to the completed apparatus, the several parts are studied in a fragmentary and disconnected manner, which necessarily fails to interest even the most inventive genius. The fact is entirely lost sight of that anatomy is a natural science, and that, like all natural sciences, it has a perfectly logical development, which ,when properly unfolded, leads the mind insensibly from the study of simple parts to their arrangement into

The Study of Physical Science—Anatomy.

complex forms, as is abundantly illustrated in the science of botany, or chemistry, or biology. But neither text-books on anatomy nor teachers of this fundamental branch of a medical education adopt the natural system of teaching this science. On the contrary, the scheme of study is so arranged as to prevent associated relations, and hence continuity of thought, on the part of the student. Therefore, he is constantly required to memorize abstract facts having no necessary connection with each other. Take, for example, the experience of a medical student in attendance at one of our most advanced medical colleges during the last year: He states that his first lesson in anatomy was a description of the external parts of the clavicle; the second was a similar description of the scapula; the third was a similar study of the femur. Meantime he had learned nothing of the structure of bones, nor of their purposes in the skeleton. When questioned, he was found to be impressed with the belief that his success as a student depended solely upon his ability to retain and promptly repeat the terms which he found in his textbook. The wonderful organism which he was studying had no more attractions for him than would a language. to a student who, in learning it, was required first to commit its dictionary to memory. The prevalent method of pursuing anatomy might be compared to the study of a cotton mill, by beginning with a spindle, and learning all of its parts, than examining a distant wheel, and committing to memory every minute detail of its construction, next learning all the peculiar names of a section of its framework, and thus proceeding until the entire machine had been studied in detached fragments. It is evident that no student would become thoroughly interested in such a study, nor would his knowledge of the machinery make him an expert engineer. He might be able to answer every question involving mere book terms,

The Place of the Bible in Education

and yet have very little useful or usable information if he were called upon to remedy defects in its machinery.

"But an experience of many years in teaching anatomy convinced me that a course of study may be followed which will thoroughly interest the average student from the first, and enable him readily to acquire, and firmly to retain in his memory, the minutest details of function and structure of tissues. How then should anatomy be studied? I answer, precisely as you would begin, continue, and finish the study of any other mechanism with the structure and functions of which you wished to become as familiar as was the inventor. It is evident that to obtain such accurate knowledge of any machine you must study it along the lines pursued by the inventor in the development of its several parts. This would require that you should place yourselves in such relations to him as to think his thought from his first conception of the needs of such an apparatus or organism to its completion in the perfected instrument. And herein lies the charm and fascination in the study of anatomy, if you adopt that logical method which the inventor pursues in the creation of a machine. From the very beginning of your studies you would be led to think the thought of the Creator, and as the wonderful mechanism of the human body was gradually unfolded, you would become more and more inspired with the loftiest conceptions of the divine wisdom and power. The psalmist, in contemplating the evidence of design in creation, sang, 'How precious also are Thy thoughts unto me, O God! how great is the sum of them!'

"It can not be doubted that the best instructor of a person who is about to study a machine so thoroughly that he can become its engineer would be the inventor himself, for while describing his own work, he would naturally become very enthusiastic and give the most accurate and detailed account of the inception, development, and completion of his invention. As the student followed the

The Study of Physical Science—Anatomy.

train of thought, he would catch the inspiration of the inventor, and as each new feature of the structure gradually developed in orderly and logical succession, his mind would be aglow with the enthusiasm of his teacher, and he would be insensibly transformed into an inventor, architect, creator, and, quite unconsciously, the thing studied would become his own. Such a scheme would lead the student to begin with the inventor's first conception of the machine about to be invented. That conception is always preceded by a recognition of a function to be performed, and the absence of any apparatus or organism to perform it. In other words, the universal law governing inventions requires that the function to be performed must first be recognized before the structure is devised. The history of every invention shows that it grew out of a recognized need of a machine to accomplish a given object, and that in its construction each part was so devised that, while it performed a special function of its own, it contributed a force or factor to the completed mechanism necessary to the successful performance of its grand purpose. We may, and should, apply the same method to the study of the structure of the human body. We should first recognize fully the function to be performed before we undertake to construct the apparatus adapted to its performance. Herein lies the secret of the successful invention of every useful mechanism. The student who enters upon and steadily pursues the study of anatomy in this spirit is from the first an inventor, and is constantly recognizing functions to be performed. and is as constantly bending all his energies to devise structural appliances to perform those functions. He not only enters into the thoughts of the Creator, but he becomes himself a creator. Thus a genuine inspiration stimulates every inventive faculty of his mind, and instead of being a mere passive agent, receiving and storing away in his memory dry and often worthless technical terms, he becomes an aggressive inquirer and explorer in this new field of science.

"Now, a course of study of anatomy so arranged that the student is from the first brought into such immediate relations with the Creator of the human mechanism that he will think His thoughts, presupposes that the Creator entered upon, proceeded with, and concluded His work according to the methods which govern all inventions. That is, the Creator discovered a want in creation, a function unperformed, and forthwith proceeded to invent an instrument to meet that want and perform that function. In adopting this theory, we must assume the direct creation of man as a new and original creature, specifically adapted in every structure for a given purpose, and our study must be along the lines already indicated viz.: First of all learn the function to be performed by this new creation, and then follow the development of structure to its completion in the perfected organism.

"The criticism which will be made upon this scheme of study is evident. It will be alleged that we ignore the modern theory of evolution, and thus inculcate antiquated ideas in regard to creation, which are liable to mislead the student. In defence of the method it may be said that the same result can be reached by adhering to the doctrine of evolution, but the scheme would necessarily be intricate and involved to such an extent as to be confusing to the average medical student. Besides, the terms of creation are used because they are more suggestive of the facts of anatomy than any terms that may be devised. Perhaps the most important testimony in favor of this method of teaching anatomy is that given by Professor Huxley, the greatest advocate of the theory of evolution. In one of his later lectures, describing the process of development of an ovum as the several stages are seen to succeed each other in symmetrical order under a powerful microscope, he is reported as saying:—

The Study of Physical Science—Anatomy.

"'Strange possibilities lie dormant in that semifluid globe. Let a moderate supply of warmth reach its watery cradle, and the plastic matter undergoes changes so rapid, and yet so steady and purpose-like in their succession, that we can only compare them to those operated by a skilled operator on a formless lump of clay. We see, as it were, a skilled modeler shaping the plastic mass with a trowel; as if a delicate finger traced out the line to be occupied by the spinal column and molded the contour of the body, pinching up the head at one end and the tail at the other, and fashioning flank and limb into the salamandrine proportions in so artistic a way that, after watching the process hour by hour, one is almost involuntarily possessed by the notion that some more subtle aid to vision than an achromatic would show the hidden artist with his plan before him, striving with skillful manipulation to perfect his work.'

"A very distinguished writer refers to this quotation as follows:—

"'The above are Huxley's own words That is to say that the first biologist in Europe (according to Virchow), when he comes to describe the development of life, can only do so in *terms of creation.*'

"With these explanatory remarks, I propose to develop the outlines of a course of study of anatomy based on the 'Terms of Creation.' If we approach the subject as inventors, and that is the true spirit in which we entered upon this study, our first inquiry would be as to the origin of the conception that man should be created. That is. What were the conditions existing which required the creation of man? We might, perhaps, arrive at a correct conclusion if we analyzed his existing organism, but, as in the Bible narrative, there is a statement of the immediate cause of his creation, and as this is the only record of the kind in human history, and answers our purpose, we will adopt it.

The Place of the Bible in Education

"Referring then to the account of creation as given in Genesis, we learn that the earth had been prepared for living things, and in an orderly manner there had appeared grass, the herb, the fruit tree. living creatures in the waters, winged fowls, cattle and creeping things and beasts of the earth, and the Creator pronounced everything good. But now there seems to have been a pause in creation, and, as we follow the narrative, we learn it was discovered that there 'was not a man to till the ground' or 'replenish the earth and subdue it' or 'have dominion' over it. Here was a new incentive to creative energy, and apparently a more difficult task was never presented even to Omnipotence. The conclusion of the deliberations of the Council of Creation are given in the announcement, 'Let Us make man in Our image, after Our likeness.' This is the first recorded mention of man in the history of the earth. The decision is in the language of a council of architects, inventors, or creations. As students, we are at once interested in determining how this man was made in the image and likeness of the Creator. On examining the record, we learn only that the Creator 'formed man of the dust of the ground, and breathed into his nostrils the breath of life.' No details are given of the method of procedure in constructing the human body, and we are left to determine these facts by our knowledge of the laws governing the invention and construction of machinery, and an analytical and synthetical study of the completed organism as we have it before us. That is, we must place ourselves as nearly as possible in line with the logical thoughts of the Inventor, and thus have the machine develop in our own studies as it did in His.

"In regard to the laws of invention, we have stated that the first conception in the inventor's mind is function, the second structure. Having recognized the former, we are now to devise and create a structure adapted to perform that function. What rule shall be our guide!—Evidently

The Study of Physical Science—Anatomy.

the rules governing construction in all inventions. These rules may be stated as follows: Every inventor creates, first, the frame-work; second, the apparatus which operates it; third, the motor power or force which gives the apparatus energy or activity; fourth, the mechanism by which the life and the integrity of the organism is to be maintained; fifth, the organs by which the machine, as a whole, is to be reproduced.

"Following the order of invention, we must determine what is the framework of the body, and begin construction with it. It is evident, on a general survey of the several tissues of the human organism, that the articulated bones make its framework or skeleton, for all the other tissues and organs are gathered about or are attached to it or concealed and protected within its recesses. We must, therefore, conclude that creative energy began the work of construction with the skeleton, and that this structure must be the first to receive our attention.

"But how is he to construct the skeleton without a perfect knowledge of the materials of which it is composed? This inquiry leads the student at once to an exhaustive study of the intimate nature of bone, for a knowledge of these facts must precede actual constructive work. Turning to the articulated skeleton as an object-lesson to learn the principal functions of bones, he notices that: First, they must sustain great weight, and, second, they must act as levers in all of the movements of the body. As an architect, he knows that the structural peculiarities necessary to the performance of these functions are: (1) Hardness, to sustain weight; (2) lightness, to facilitate movement; (3) elasticity, to resist violence. Here are three nearly opposite qualities to be combined in one tissue, and his curiosity is intensely excited to discover the thoughts of the Divine Architect as He proceeds to solve the difficult problem. But we will not follow the student in his study of osteology, or the science of bone. We assume that every phase in its development from the selection of its constituent materials to their final organization must interest one who is seeking as an inventor to determine its adaptation to the purpose for which it is created. He can but marvel at the wisdom that takes certain salts of the earth and combines them with a peculiar kind of animal matter in such manner that these heterogeneous substances by some unknown and unknowable affinity create a new substance having the qualities of hardness, lightness, and elasticity; qualities essential to bone in the performance of its varied functions in the skeleton. Scarcely less wonderful to him is the development of bone from the osteal cell and the conversion of the body of the cell into a lakelet, through the medium of which the new bone is nourished by hydrostatic pressure. And as he follows the formation of bone to its completion, he discovers in the construction of its tissue the demonstration of two new and very important principles in physics. The first is that a hollow cylinder is stronger than a solid shaft of the same size. This principle applied in mechanics economizes the materials employed and renders the structure comparatively light, thus adding to facility of movement. The result is beautifully illustrated in the long bones or levers of the skeleton. The second principle is the Gothic arch, which gives the greatest power of sustaining weight with the least amount of material; the greatest elasticity with the highest degree of lightness.

"Having completed a minute study of bone and obtained an accurate knowledge of its constituents, its methods of development, and the structural arrangements adapting it to its various purposes, the student is prepared to advance to the actual construction of bones, and of placing each in its proper position in the skeleton.

"Surveying the skeleton as a whole, the question again arises, Where shall constructive work begin? In other words, Which series of bones was first created? His answer

The Study of Physical Science—Anatomy.

must be determined by recalling the principle of construction of all machinery, viz., the central or axial part must be made first. Applying this principle as he critically examines the articulated bones, his attention is at once arrested by the series which constitute the spinal column as not only central in location, but obviously the other bones are attached to it in such a manner as to prove that they depend upon it in the performance of their functions. He is warranted, therefore, in concluding that the spinal column must have been the part of the skeleton which first received the attention of the Creator.

"But this conclusion does not solve the question as to the initial point where construction began, for the spinal column is constituted of many bones. He has decided as to the series of bones first constructed, but he has not fixed upon the individual bone in the series. In selecting that bone, he must again determine which is the most central and important as regards function. It must be noted that in this view a vertebra proper includes the corresponding ribs and their sternal attachments, as described by Professor Owen in his great work on 'Vertebrates.' In that system, 'each complete segment, called "vertebra," consists of a series of osseous pieces arranged according to a type or general plan, in which they form a hoop or arch above and another beneath a central piece; the upper hoop, encircling a segment of the nervous axis, is called the neural arch; the lower hoop encircling a part of the vascular system, is called the haemal arch; their common center is termed the centrum.' A vertebra, thus defined, he calls a 'type segment,' and the skeleton of his ideal, or 'archetype' vertebrate, consists of a series of these perfectly-formed segments as we see them in the skeleton of a serpent.

"As the student critically examines the different vertebrae to determine with which the Creator began construction, he is impressed with the important fact that, while the segments of the spinal column have a general resemblance to each other, as if constructed after one model, there are differences which become more and more marked when those of either extremity of the column are contrasted with those in the central or dorsal region. This region must be the point of departure in construction. On examining critically each vertebra to determine which is the 'type segment,' his selection falls upon the seventh dorsal, for all its-parts are more complete than any other, and its ribs are longer and more perfectly adapted to their functions. With the *seventh dorsal*, therefore, he concludes that construction must begin.

"Taking this vertebra in hand to begin practical work, the student at once discovers that it is constituted of many individual parts, each adapted to its special function. Again, he must determine which part is the center or axis of the vertebra before he can positively decide where the construction work originally began, and hence where he is to commence his operations. Examining very carefully the several parts of a vertebra, and comparing it with the others in the series he notices that the body is the most important portion, for not only are the other parts arranged around and connected with it as a base of action, but it is the only constituent of a vertebra which is continuous throughout the entire spinal column. The body, therefore, or centrum, must have been first created. By this process of scientific inquiry and logical reasoning he reaches at last the initial point where the Creator actually began the work of constructing the human mechanism, viz., *the centrum of the seventh dorsal vertebra.*

"Here, then, the student begins the actual study of what is, in a real sense, 'practical anatomy.' The seventh dorsal vertebra is the point of departure from which he is to develop, in serial order, not only the skeleton, but the entire human organism. The science of anatomy, like kindred natural sciences, thus has its beginnings in a few

The Study of Physical Science—Anatomy.

simple principles or conditions, and out of them grow the complex forms which are so difficult to understand when studied independently and without a previous thorough knowledge of these fundamental facts.

"As the student, now fully equipped for his task. begins constructive study, we may well regard him as Huxley's 'skilled operator on a formless lump of clay;' 'a skilled modeler shaping the plastic mass;' 'the hidden artist with his plan before him, striving with skillful manipulation to perfect his work.' The plan before him is the articulated skeleton, and the materials are the individual bones; the former for synthetical study or the placing of each bone in its proper position, and the latter for analytical study, or the minute examination of its technical peculiarities. His method is still that of an inventor and creator, for he will learn the nature of the function before he begins structural work. Having found the initial point of construction of the mechanism which he is about to create, and being thoroughly familiar with the rules governing his art, our artist-student, our 'skilled modeler,' 'with his plan before him,' enters upon his task with enthusiasm, and pursues his studies with ever-increasing delight. We see him model with nicest skill the interior of the body of the seventh dorsal vertebra, filling it with Gothic arches that it may sustain great weight and still be very light. No sculptor's chisel ever wrought in marble more artistic curves than those which he gives to the exterior covering With 'delicate fingers' he shapes the neural arch, 'pinching up' the terminal portions of the laminae to form the graceful spinous process. With mathematical exactness he cuts the articulating facets so as to secure a minimum of motion with a maximum of strength. For the haemal arch he forms the ribs and curves them so that they shall perform the twofold function of protecting the organs of the chest and aiding in respiration through their nicely-adjusted articulations with the body and lateral processes. He finishes the haemal arch with the costal cartilages and the sternum and, adjusting the several parts to each other, the seventh vertebra, the 'type-segment,' stands forth perfect in all its details, a beautiful specimen of high art. With its completion the student has acquired the key to a thorough knowledge of all the bones of the skeleton, for the remaining bones are but variations of the seventh dorsal, the 'type-segment.' And all of these variations from the seventh are simply designed to adapt other vertebra to new functions. Hence he proceeds with comparative ease in his constructive study of the spinal column below and above the seventh dorsal. As he descends, he modifies each vertebra according to its function, until he reaches the coccyx, where he preserves only a remnant of the body. As he ascends from the seventh dorsal, more remarkable changes take place, as in the atlas and axis, but most strikingly in the bones of the skull and face. But in these irregular and curiously-formed bones the 'student-artist' recognizes only variations of the 'type-segment,' adapting parts or the whole of the vertebra to new functions. Even in the bones of the upper and lower extremities he discovers two vertebrae which have undergone extreme variations owing to the peculiar functions they have to perform.

"Thus in our scheme of study the seventh dorsal represents the 'Vertebrate Archetype' of Owen, which Holden says is 'the grammar of all osteology.' He adds, 'Of this a student may rest assured, that however minutely he may have scrutinized the bones. he can not *understand* them unless he knows something of the vertebrate archetype; without this knowledge he is like one who speaks a language fluently, but is ignorant of its grammar.' And we may add that he has acquired a chain of associated facts which will remain indelibly impressed upon his memory, and that will enable him to recall promptly the function and the structural peculiarities of every bone in all the emergencies of practise.

The Study of Physical Science—Anatomy.

"Having completed the skeleton or framework, our artist-student recognizes that it must be endowed with at least two forces to enable the coming man to perform the task of tilling the earth and subduing it. First, he must have the power of locomotion, or of moving from place to place, and, second, he must have the power of prehension, or of seizing and holding objects. In construction the student must have noticed that the bones were designed to move upon one another, and that those of the extremities take the form of levers. The question now before him is as to the kind of apparatus to be constructed to operate these levers, and how it is to be applied. Holding up before my class the seventh and sixth dorsal vertebrae in proper position, I asked, 'How would you make these bones move on each other?' A first-course student replied, 'Attach a rubber strap to their spinous processes.' He stated a principle and a fact; the principle was that the apparatus with which one bone is to be moved upon another must have the quality of contraction, and the fact was that such a strap as he suggested, though not made of rubber, was already attached to their spinous processes. The incident illustrates the readiness of the student, whose mind is trained to devise structures adapted to perform functions, to anticipate the very existence and nature of the tissues which he is about to study. It serves also to accentuate the proposition that I then made to the effect that, as these central dorsal bones were first constructed, according to our scheme of creation, we may logically conclude that to these bones were applied the first structures made to move the levers of the body. Here, then, at the seventh dorsal, we find the *type muscle*, and here we begin our constructive study of the muscular system.

"Preparatory for constructive work, the student must now acquire, first, an accurate knowledge of the histological peculiarities of muscles and of their classification, and, second, he must practically learn the nature and

The Place of the Bible in Education

classification of levers—two most interesting subjects to the inventor, and which, thoroughly understood, give to the surgeon great practical skill.

"Assuming that he has acquired this knowledge, he begins the study of muscles *in situ*. He must reject altogether the method pursued in the text-books, which follows the order of dissections; for nothing could be more unscientific than to construct the muscles beginning with the most superficial layer and finishing with the deepest muscles. Now the order of creation must necessarily have been the very reverse of this. If we apply the muscles with our own fingers, as I propose, we must place the deepest layer first and the superficial layer last. This method has this obvious advantage, that the deepest muscles are usually simple and have a single action, while the superficial muscles are compound and complex in form and action.

"It will be alleged that this method of study necessitates delaying dissections until the student has completed the review of the entire muscular system as given in the text-books. It is true that he would have to learn the muscles of a part, as the trunk or a limb, from his book before he attempted its dissection. And there is this advantage in such an order of studying, that his dissection will be much more carefully and intelligently made if he has already a correct knowledge of the parts he is now practically demonstrating.

"Recurring now to the adaptation of muscles to the levers of the skeleton to give the latter functional activity, the question again arises in the mind of the artist-students as to the point where he is to begin. In other words, 'Which muscle in the order of creation was first applied?' Logically, the first bone created,—the seventh dorsal, according to our scheme,—would receive the first attention. Now the articulations of this bone show that it has a

The Study of Physical Science—Anatomy.

limited motion on the adjoining vertebrae, and to effect that motion the greatest leverage would be secured by attaching a muscle to the spinous processes of the two bones, as suggested by the student. He was thinking the thoughts of the Creator, for we find in the interspinales muscles the identical elastic cords that he the recognized as necessary for the performance of the first and simplest function of these bones. These simple structures, so small in the dorsal region, but so well developed in the cervical, may be taken as the first muscles applied.

"Commencing then with the *interspinalis muscle of the seventh dorsal vertebra*, as the point of departure in the study of the muscular system, the student follows the line of constructive thought in the most natural and scientific manner to the final application of the last muscle to the terminal bones of the extremities. Throughout this entire study his dominant thought as an inventor is in each case, 'What class of muscles must I select? and where shall I attach them to the bones to enable them to perform the functions for which they were severally created?' Thus, as the skeleton developed from a single central thought, so the muscular system now grows under his plastic hand in symmetrical form from the little, delicate slip that he placed between the spinous processes of the seventh dorsal and its neighbor to the enormous, intricate, and complex erector spinae, multifidus and complexus, muscles of the back which students, following the old method of study, usually group very properly under the term '*musculus perplexus*.' Having completed the muscles of the trunk, he proceeds to apply them to the great levers of the extremities. In this part of his study all his inventive faculties are inspired with the keenest insight by the revelation of the marvelous forms of adaptation of muscular force to effect the infinite variety of motions of these levers. And the one fact that perhaps will impress him most is this, that all these muscles, even to the terminal phalanges, have as the basis of their action the spinal column, and chiefly the central dorsal vertebra where he began the study of both the skeleton and the muscular system. This arrangement and action of the muscles will appear as he traces the peculiar relations of one muscle to another, beginning with the spinal column and terminating with the extreme bones of either limb. Though in the series there may be several muscles, each having its special function when acting alone, yet it is evident that they may all act together as a compound muscle, and perform a new and quite independent action. This is strikingly illustrated by Professor Owen in the figure of a man stooping under a heavy load, which rests upon his shoulders. The weight is sustained chiefly by the following muscles, viz., the erector spinae of the back, the glutei at the hips, the quadriceps extensors of the thigh, the gastrocnemii of the legs, and the short flexors of the feet. Here are ten separate and independent muscles, extending from the spine to the ends of the toes, now united in their action to perform one function.

"In the construction of the human organism we have now completed the framework and the apparatus which is to operate it. But as yet we have only an inert and inanimate object, quite incapable of performing the duties for which it was created. Our next inquiry as inventors must be, 'How shall these muscles be endowed with force and these dry bones be stimulated to activity?' The result of creative thought and energy was the development of that marvelous and exquisitely beautiful mechanism the nervous system. Studying along the lines of creation, the dullest student becomes fascinated with the wonderful adaptation of means to an end which he discovers in every part of this system, but especially in the nerve-centers, where the power is generated which moves the muscles to action. As in the study of the skeleton and muscular system the student learned the intimate nature of bone and

The Study of Physical Science—Anatomy.

muscle before beginning construction, so now the histological peculiarities of the materials constituting the nerve tissue are thoroughly learned, and the special uses of each kind or form are fully understood. Then constructive work begins, and the point of departure is again the seventh dorsal, because here is found the *type nerve-center* of which all others are only variations to meet special functions. This one nerve-center, thoroughly analyzed and understood, is the key to a ready appreciation of the peculiarities of every other, as was a knowledge of the seventh dorsal vertebra a key to a quick understanding of the special features of every other bone of the skeleton. Even in the complicated and complex forms of nerve centers of the brain the student readily recognizes the special variations of the 'type nerve-center' made to meet new functions, and so appreciates the necessity of the changes that he forever retains them in his memory. Not less interesting when studied in order is the origin of nerves from the centers, the method of distribution through the medium of a plexus, their final termination in muscles and other tissues, and their relations, in their courses, to other tissues.

"We have now reviewed the construction of three great systems of tissues,—the osseous for a framework of the mechanism, the muscular to operate it, and the nervous to give it energy. But it is apparent to us as inventors that this machine, being subject to 'wear and tear,' and hence to decay and death, must not only be supplied with the means of repairing waste, but of perpetuating itself when its life ends. These facts open new fields for constructive study, and the artist-student begins with renewed zeal to trace in his plan the origin and development of the digestive system, then its auxiliary, the circulatory system, and finally, the reproductive system.

"We need not follow the student farther. He continues his study and construction along the lines of original thought, always first recognizing a function to be performed before he studies the apparatus designed to perform it. As he proceeds, all the details of the mechanism unfold in the logical order peculiar to the natural sciences, 'pointing,' says Holden, 'to the one great Cause of all organization.'

"A student who has in this manner thoroughly mastered the several systems of tissues theoretically finds their demonstration by dissection a constant source of delight. Every stroke of the scalpel is made with precision, and reveals a hidden thought of the Creator in new and living light, which engraves upon the memory of the dissector the details of function and structure so distinctly that, at all times and in all emergencies, this knowledge is immediately available. And I may add, as a final statement, that to the philosophical, devout, and creative mind, seeking knowledge along these lines of inquiry, the ecstatic remark of Galen is eminently true, *"The study of anatomy is a perpetual hymn to the gods."'*

Chapter 17.

The Study of Physical Science—Healing.

FURTHER in the medical field there can be read from the Bible the *text*, "The inhabitant shall not say, I am sick: the people that dwell therein shall be forgiven their iniquity," revealing the *principle* that *sin* is a vital element in physical sickness, and that consequently the *forgiveness of sin*, which involves the ceasing to sin the cutting off of sin by righteousness, is a thing to be recognized and employed in the Christian treatment of disease. Proceeding upon this principle, it can confidently be declared and forever taught, as has been declared and taught by the editor of *American Medicine*, George M. Gould, M. D.:—

>"The relationship of sin and disease has been recognized by all great philosophic minds, but nowhere has it been so accurately expressed as in the treuchant words of Cotton Mather, who speaks of disease as '*Flagellum Dei pro peccaiis mundi.*' To those modern materialists, or atheists, and especially to the all-knowing agnostics, who misuse science for dogmatic purposes, this saying of Cotton Mather will seem beneath their scorn, because to their thinking there is neither sin nor God. They should go one step further, and with their allies, the unchristian scientists, make 'an end on't' by also denying the existence of disease and the world. It is an old trick of the mind to rid one's self of difficulties and responsibilities by denying the existence of facts. *He who silences his conscience by denying sin, only adds another sin to his individual burden, and another sinner to the burden of the*

The Place of the Bible in Education

world....Let us therefore assume as beyond discussion that atheism is unscientific, and that God lives, and that *sin is opposing and not furthering His biologic work in the world*...

"God is a true physician, working for final normality. He may cauterize in order to cure, and prefer amputation rather than necrosis. His patient is the entire future body an soul of humanity, not the individual members now and here existing. The wise ones of the world, the philosophers and the prophets, the leaders of men to better living, have been those who saw the far and subtle lines and laws of causation running back from disease and untimely death to *the sources of ignorance (which is also sin), of selfishness, and of wrong-doing.* This is the text of all preaching and prophecy, the burthen of all tragedy, the plot of all literature. *And it is the heart of medicine!*...As physicians we must work to cure and prevent disease. If, as we have seen, disease is always more or less dependent upon sin, we must in a scientific prophylaxis try to stop the sin that partly or entirely generates or allows the disease....

"Science, it is plain, has outrun morality; we know how to lengthen the average human life by many years, with a proportionate reduction of all the suffering and expense, but we are powerless to do it. because, *simply of sin.* There is no doubt that sin alone prevents a reduction of the death rate and sickness by one-half, and a lengthening of life to 50 or 60 years. *And we have nearly or quite reached the limit so far as the art of therapeutics is concerned.* We can never cure a much greater proportion of the sick until we have *better bodies and souls in the patients.* The great progress of the future in medicine will be prevention. We must lose our life to find it. There are about 1,500,000 deaths annually in the United States—at least 500,000 more than there would be if we could carry out sanitary reforms of proved efficacy....There is no prevention of disease without stifling the causes of disease. *Wherever sin exists, it works itself out finally in sickness and death.* The man who says his sole duty is to cure disease, not to bother about sin or society, is a bad physician and a poor

The Study of Physical Science—Healing.

citizen. In a hundred ways he can influence his neighbors and his nation, to lessen disease and death, besides by what the text-books call therapeutics. *The best therapeutics is to render therapeutics unnecessary.*"

This idea of the forgiveness of sins as an element in the true treatment of disease does not in any sense sanction the quackery of the so-called faith-cures. Undeniably, faith is in it: because forgiveness of sins is received and known only by means of faith. But it is the "faith which works;" not an airy, figmentary "faith" that prays and "believes" and sits around and does nothing. It is the faith which upon the Word of God and the love of God teaches the forgiveness of sins and then works most vigorously to reduce fever, to eliminate poisons, and diligently to search for the physical causes of the sickness, in order that these causes shall with the sins be forever abandoned, and the true way of true health, which is inseparable from holiness be faithfully followed in the future.

Upon this principle the philosophy of the forgiveness of sins is studied in order to *know how*, as a matter of practical knowledge, the forgiveness of sins enters as an element into practical medical science. And in this direction there is not far to go to find at least one important truth as to how this is. Here it is: "*Peace, peace* to him that is far off, and to him that is near, saith the Lord; and *I will heal him*. But the wicked are like the troubled sea, when it can not rest, whose waters cast up mire and dirt. There is no peace, saith my God, to the wicked." Isa. 57:19–21. The peace of God which comes to man in the forgiveness of sins and the restoration of the soul to righteousness is a distinct element in recovery from sickness, and is a right of way to health. And there is not an intelligent physician in the world, even though he be an avowed atheist, who will not say that a disturbed mind, troubled heart, a perplexed life, is a positive hindrance to whatever may be done to bring a

The Place of the Bible in Education

person back from sickness to health; while, on the other hand, peace of mind and quietness and rest of heart are a positive aid. And that sound medical principle, which every physician recognizes, is declared in the Bible as a medical principle; and is given by the Lord directly as a medical prescription to the sick: "*Peace, peace,*...saith the Lord; and *I will heal* him."

And yet this is but an instance in illustration of the essential virtue and power of the word of God to heal. It is written: "He sent His word, and healed them." Ps. 107:20. And of the medicinal virtue of His word as such, it is written: "My son, attend to My words; incline thine ear unto My sayings. Let them not depart from thine eyes; keep them in the midst of thine heart. For they are life unto those that find them, and *health* [margin, Heb., "medicine"] to all their"—spirit?—No. "To all their"—mind?—No. But "to all their *flesh*." It is *the flesh* that *disease* takes hold of. But the words of God received into the heart, and treasured in the life, and allowed to be indeed the spring of the life—this is "health to all the flesh." It is the Divine Physician's own prescription for health, and the Divine virtue is in it for all who will take the "medicine" thus prescribed. The prescription is repeated in Ex. 15:26 and in Deut. 7:12–15.

And yet all this is but a part of the expression of the Lord's supreme wish with respect to the health of mankind. For He says, "I wish *above all things* that thou mayest prosper and be in health." 3 John 2. Indeed, He puts His wish for the prosperity of the *health* of man exactly on an equality with His wish for the prosperity of the *soul* of man: "I wish above all things that thou mayest prosper and be in health, *even as* thy soul prospereth." And this is but the repetition of the mighty truth already touched upon, that, as the opposite of sin and disease as being inseparable, *health and holiness are inseparable.*

The Study of Physical Science—Healing.

This truth is revealed in the native English language in which we speak, and in its mother languages, as well as in the Bible. The word "health" is an abstract noun, from "*whole*," not from "*heal.*" The real meaning of the word "whole" is "hale, sound, entire, complete." The original sense of the word "whole" is "hale," which signifies "in sound health." This is confirmed by that verse of scripture, "They that be whole need not a physician, but they that are sick."

The original form of the present word "hale" is "hal." And its descent is "hal, hol, hool, hole, hwole. whole." Thus the spelling "h–a–l–e" is only a later Scandinavian form of the word "whole." The present Norwegian word for "whole" is "*hel.*" Indeed, the "w" in the word "whole" has been in use only about four hundred years; and the English Philological Society has recommended the dropping of the "w," so as to restore the word to its connection with its related words, "holy," "heal," "health," etc.

Thus the descent of our word "whole," in that line, from the original "*hal,*" shows it to mean "in sound health."

This word has another line of descent, which presents an additional and very important idea. It runs thus: hal, hol, hool, hole, holy, hole-ness, holy-ness, holi-ness; for our present word "holy" is "nothing but Middle English '*hool*' (now spelled w–h–o–l–e), with suffix 'y'." The Anglo-Saxon runs the same: "*hal,*" with suffix "*ig,*" forming "*halig.*" This suffix "ig" corresponds exactly to our modern English "y," so that the Anglo-Saxon "*halig*" is precisely our modern word "holy." Corresponding to the Anglo-Saxon "*halig*" is the German "*heilig,*" which also corresponds precisely to our present word "holy." And that German word "*heilig*" is from the word "*heil,*" which signifies "health, happiness, safety, salvation." The descent and family of the word in German is this:—

Heil, signifying hale, whole, healthy.

The Place of the Bible in Education

Heiland, signifying the Saviour, from "old present participle—the healing or saving One."

Heilig, signifying (healthful, bringing the highest welfare; hence) holy, sacred.

Heiligkeit, signifying holiness.

Heilsam, signifying wholesome, healing.

The German of Isa. 12:2 is, "*Siehe, Gott ist mein Heil....Gott der Herr ist meine Starke und mein Psalm, und ist mein Heil.*"

The Scandinavian languages—indeed, the whole Teutonic family of languages—tell the same story. And that story is that in the true conception of health both holiness and its resultant—salvation—are comprehended.

Where our further-back mother tongue says "*heil*," our immediate mother tongue says "salvation." And the Bible says that health and salvation are the same thing: "God be merciful unto us, and bless us; and cause His face to shine upon us; that *Thy way* may be known upon earth, *Thy saving health* among all nations." Ps. 67:1, 2. The health which is of God is "*saving* health." It means holiness, and salvation because of holiness. His "way" known on earth is His "saving health" known among all nations.

Again: "Why art thou cast down, O my soul? and why art thou disquieted in me? hope thou in God: for I shall yet praise Him for the help of His countenance." The Hebrew words in English letters say. "For His presence is salvation."

And, "I shall yet praise Him, who is the health of my countenance, and my God." The *help* of *His* countenance is the *health* of *my* countenance. His presence is salvation, and His presence is health. Then by the Scriptures, true salvation is health, and true health is salvation. Ps. 42:5, 11. See also Ps. 43:5.

The Study of Physical Science—Healing.

Finally: "Let us cleanse ourselves from all filthiness of the *flesh* and *spirit*, perfecting holiness in the fear of God." 2 Cor. 7:1.

What is filthiness of the flesh?—It is tobacco using; opium eating; tea, coffee, beer, or whisky drinking; eating unclean and unwholesome food; unclean habits of living. From all such things the Christian cleanses himself. But when that is done, only half of the man is reached. He must also cleanse himself from "all filthiness of the spirit:" from all uncleanness of thought and word. The man must do both to attain to true holiness, haleness, health, salvation.

Thus emphasized in the Bible and its philosophy throughout, and rooted and imbedded in the very language in which we speak, is the truth as a medical principle that health and holiness are inseparably combined. Therefore in every Christian these must also be inseparably combined: else how can we be truly and intelligently Christian? And of all things these two—health and holiness—must be inseparably combined in the physician: and only less so in the preacher. The preacher who separates them, fails to preach the principles of true holiness; and the physician who separates them, fails to practise the principles of true health. And what God has so inseparably joined together, how can any person do well in putting asunder?

TEMPERANCE: HEALTHFUL LIVING.

This unity of health and holiness involves the principle of a regard for temperance and healthful living. We have seen that this was a specific study in the schools of the prophets. We have seen that temperance was one of the prominent characteristics of the youth and, indeed, the life of Daniel. That this was taught to him in the school which he attended, and was a material part of his education before his captivity, is evident from the fact that it was already a fixed principle in his life at that time.

When the royal captives reached Babylon, "the kind appointed them a daily provision of the king's meat, and of the wine which he drank." The word here translated "meat" signifies "dainties;" and refers to the royal dainties, such as would be expected at the table of such a great king. It included flesh meats, of course; for these were largely used; but the word signifies all the royal dainties.

But Daniel refused it all, and also refused the wine, and chose "pulse to eat, and water to drink." The word translated "pulse" is a word of wide meaning, just as is the word translated "meat," referring to the king's dainties. The word translated "pulse" comprehends the whole realm of vegetarian diet, just as the other word comprehends the whole field of the King's dainties. What Daniel asked was that he, with his three companions, might have a vegetarian diet for food, and water to drink, instead of the richly-prepared and highly-seasoned dainties of the king's table for food, and his wine for drink.

This action of those four boys was but the expression of a fixed principle, derived from knowledge of the effects which the king's provision would have. For Daniel not only "purposed in his heart" that he would not partake of the king's victuals and drink, but he did this because "he would not defile himself" with those things. He refused that food and drink because he knew their defiling effect upon those who used them.

For the effect of all such food and drink is certainly to defile. To illustrate: If your lamp chimney is all befogged, the light will not shine clearly through it: not half the light will shine through it then that will shine through it when it is well cleaned. Yet the light itself within the chimney may be the same all the time. The oil may be of the purest, the wick perfectly trimmed, there may be no lack whatever in

The Study of Physical Science—Healing.

the light itself; yet if the chimney be dusty, smoky, or in any way befogged, the light will not shine clearly. It simply *can not* shine clearly, because of the condition of the medium through which it must shine.

You know that when this is so, the thing to do is *not* to tinker the light nor to find fault with it, but *to clean the chimney.* And you know that when you do clean the chimney, the light is not only *allowed* to shine through, but it is actually *enabled* to shine as it can not possibly without any chimney. Thus it is literally true that, other things being equal, the strength and clearness of the light depend upon the medium through which it must shine.

Now, believers in Christ are the mediums through which the light of God, by His Holy Spirit, must shine to the world. That light is perfect. It is impossible that there should be any lack whatever in the perfect shining of that light itself. So far as there is any lack in perfect shining, it is altogether because of defect in the medium through which the light would shine. And anything whatever that benumbs the nerves or clogs the blood, befogs the system and bedims the light of God, as certainly as that befogged lamp chimney bedims the light of the lamp.

Every kind of stimulant and narcotic—wine, tobacco, beer, coffee, tea—does benumb the nerves; and all richly-cooked, highly-seasoned, and flesh-meat food does clog the blood; so that the effect of all or any of these is to befog the system, and bedim the light of God that would shine, by His Holy Spirit, through our lives in the darkness of the world.

Daniel lived in the darkest age of ancient Israel,—the age when it fell by the weight of its own iniquity. He also lived in the darkest age of ancient Babylon,—the age when Babylon also fell by the weight of its own iniquity. Daniel stood in the world as one of the professed people of God, through whom the light of God must shine in the darkness of the world of his day.

We live today in an age that corresponds to that of both Jerusalem and Babylon. Today God calls His people out of Babylon, that they "be not partakers of her sins," and "receive not of her plagues." We stand as the professed people of God, through whom the light must shine in the darkness of the world. Yet hundreds, we fear there are thousands, of professed Christians do drink tea, coffee, or other such evil stuff, and do habitually eat flesh meats, dainties, and highly-seasoned food; and then wonder why their neighbors do not "see the light"! They ask the Lord for His Holy Spirit, and then wonder why they have "so little influence"!

The truth is, their neighbors can not see the light: it is so bedimmed by their befogged minds and lives that people simply *can not* see it clearly. The Lord gives His Holy Spirit, He has now poured out His Holy Spirit; the perfect light is given, and as for the light itself, it *can not* shine any clearer; but this holy light is bedimmed by the benumbed nerves and befogged senses of these users of tea, coffee, flesh meats, and dainties, so that even those who long to see it, and are looking earnestly for it can not see it. It *can not* shine to them.

Daniel would not so defile himself. He had respect to the claims of his profession of being one of God's people. He therefore cleansed himself "from all filthiness of the flesh and spirit," that the light of God might shine undimmed and unhindered by the medium through which that light must shine in the darkness where he was. And all this happened for an example, and it is written for our admonition, upon whom the ends of the world are come. Please, then, do not any more dare to sing, "Dare to be a Daniel," unless you do really dare to be a Daniel.

The Study of Physical Science—Healing.

Nobody had any difficulty in seeing the light where Daniel and his companions were. It shone clearly. The moral integrity which they had acquired through the Word and Spirit of God shed its clear, distinct rays in every situation in which they were found. The light of this single principle of temperance and right living shone so clearly and so powerfully, in these boys, in contrast with the others, as to win the approval of the king's high officer. Dan. 1:12–15.

All this is precisely what is wanted today in the darkness of the Babylon that surrounds us. Who of those today who profess to have the light of God for the world will defile themselves with the Babylonish meats and drinks of those around them? Who today, of all these, will not, in deed and in truth, "dare to be a Daniel"?

Chapter 18.

The Study of Physical Science—Physical Culture.

PHYSICAL culture is a phase of education that excites much interest. And, like other features of education, it is carried on by methods as far as possible from those of true education. True physical culture is manual training, or industrial education. It is the training or educating of all the faculties to do expert work in honest and useful occupations: while the popular physical culture is devoted solely to the training of muscular powers to the winning point in games, races, and all sorts of contest of physical strength and endurance. And in this difference there lies a world of meaning.

Christianity requires honest work at honest and useful occupations: as it is written: "Even when we were with you, this we commanded you, that if any would not work, neither should he eat. For we hear that there are some which walk among you disorderly, working not at all, but are busybodies. Now them that are such we command and exhort by our Lord Jesus Christ, that with quietness they work, and eat their own bread." 2 Thess. 3:10–12. "Let ours also learn to profess honest trades for necessary uses, that they be not unfruitful." Titus 3:14, margin. "Let him that stole steal no more: but rather let him labor, working with his hands the thing which is good, that he may have to give to him that needeth." Eph. 4:28.

The one model Christian and model Man has set the example of all Christianity. And counting from the time

The Place of the Bible in Education

that He was twelve years old in the flesh to the time of His baptism when He entered specifically upon His teaching and ministry, He spent nearly six times as much of His life on earth in the daily occupation of manual labor as He spent in the direct work of His public ministry. Now it can not be said that He learned that trade and spent this time at it with the expectation that He would or might need it afterward "some time" as a means of "making a living." This therefore demonstrates that in manual labor, honest work at honest occupation, there is that which is valuable to man for *itself alone*: that in itself it is an end, and not merely a means to an end.

It is therefore an utter mistake for anybody to think that manual labor is in any sense a curse, or any part of the curse. Yet it can not be denied that multitudes of men think that such labor is akin to a curse, if not the very original curse itself. Indeed, even many Christians so misread the Word of God as to make it appear that the requirement that man shall eat bread by the sweat of his face is a material part of the curse. It is not so. The word of God to man is, "Cursed is *the ground* for *thy sake*....In the sweat of thy face shalt thou eat bread." When some *thing* is cursed *for* MY SAKE, then the cursing of that *thing* is to *me* not a curse, but a *blessing*. For that which is done for my sake is an evidence of a special thought, care, and consideration for me: and of good-will to me. And such is the wise provision that "In the sweat of thy face shalt thou eat bread."

When the man was created and put in the garden, it was with the purpose that He should work. For it is observed that before he was made "there was not a man to till the ground." And when he was made, God "put him into the garden of Eden *to dress it* and *to keep it*." Gen. 2:5, 15. Thus industrial occupation was an essential to the welfare of man in his very creation, and in paradise, with the purpose that he should enjoy that blissful place and state forevermore. And when this was essential to the welfare of man in

The Study of Physical Science—Physical Culture.

righteousness, perfection, and paradise, only the more is it essential when he has fallen into sin and imperfection. Therefore in this latter state, since work is the more needed for his welfare, *for his sake* the ground is caused to require more labor in the dressing and keeping of it so that it shall supply to man the needed sustenance.

Yet more than this, there is in it a *moral element*. While the man was sinless, there were in the earth no untoward elements; and his occupation was only, in its perfect and blessed abundance of all that was good, to dress it and to keep it. But after the man had fallen into sin, and when God would save him from the sin, increase of occupation is required. And though it is now actual *labor* and this to the extent of "the sweat of his face," yet it is all "for his sake." And all of this reveals the mighty truth that work, manual labor, industrial occupation, holds an important place as an element in the recovery from the inroad of sin, and in the development of morals. And this view is clearly confirmed by the lily of Christ on earth. It is therefore in the perfect strictness of truth and philosophy that the word stands, "Cursed is the ground *for thy sake*....In the sweat of thy face shalt thou eat bread."

But in his darkness and perversion of mind man naturally sees things in the reverse. It is therefore the natural inclination of men not to work if they can help it: to work only when they have to, and then only as far as possible to get themselves into a position or condition where they can live without work. They will spend much money and time in the taking of lessons in athletics, in violent exertion in games of all sorts, in vigorous and systematic motions for exercise and for health; but they will not work. Manual labor, industrial occupation, they despise as something disgraceful to their sort; for *they* "do not have to work."

The Place of the Bible in Education

This persistent tendency to avoid work, and to indulge in desperate contests in games and races, is today industriously cultivated in popular education The course thus taken is both a positive detriment to the youth and a menace to society itself. This truth is confirmed by the unerring evidence produced by the camera. In the photographs of contestants in bicycle races, for instance, taken at the crucial point of the race at the winning line, when every faculty of the being is swallowed up in the contest, it has been discovered that in the facial expression there is remarkable sameness; and that that which is revealed in these countenances is the very intensity of all the worst passions of the human soul. The expression of hatred, variance, emulation, wrath, strife, envy, jealousy, malignity, murder, fear, horror, despair, make them almost as the faces of demons rather than of men.

There is a better education than that. There is a better physical culture than that. For this reason alone, if there were no others, every Christian school absolutely excludes all games and all contests and rivalry of every kind, either intellectual or physical. In the place of these, the Christian school establishes useful industrial occupations for the employment of all students. Actual work in these occupations is made an essential part of the education which the school supplies, and for which the student pays; and no person will be received as a student nor employed as a teacher who will not willingly go to the work in these occupations in the work hours, as to the work in books in the hours of study or recitation.

The Christian school will not countenance anything that will in any way suggest that there is any distinction between work and education: it will steadily and uncompromisingly hold that work is education, and education is work. The Christian school will not recognize the view that work is a means *to* an education in the sense that a person can work his way to an education, and when he has

The Study of Physical Science—Physical Culture.

obtained his education he can consider himself above such work. The Christian school will allow that work is a means to an education only in the single sense that the work itself is education: that true education is found in the very work itself. Therefore for such a school to employ teachers to instruct only in the recitation rooms, and occupy themselves with the students only in recitation hours, while the students themselves must occupy themselves in recitation hours and work hours besides—this would be only to sanction in the strongest way, by example, that there is a clear distinction between education and work, so that, when a person has education sufficient to be able to teach, he may properly be considered to be exempt from work. That would be an abandonment of the principle, and putting in its place a mere theory.

Another important principle involved in this is that the Christian school, like all other Christian things. can go on forever: no long vacations are ever needed. Long vacations are in themselves a detriment, unless the time out of school is spent in some useful employment. But when all the time in school is properly balanced between manual labor and book study, educational effort is not so one-sided that it is necessary to abandon it for several months in order for the system of the student to regain its proper balance. Combined with God's great blessing of physical labor—honest work at honest trades and occupations—to invigorate the body, educational efforts in Christian schools, instead of ever becoming wearisome tasks, are continually reviving inspirations, and can go on daily forever as easily as to go on at all.

Thus in every way there is true science and philosophy in God's great blessing of manual labor in Christian schools as well as everywhere else. And in view of the truth of God's Word on the subject, how can any school be truly Christian that willingly despises or neglects this truly Christian physical culture?

Chapter 19.

The Study of Physical Science—*Continued*.

ASTRONOMY must be a study in Christian schools, in obedience to the call of the Lord, "Lift up your eyes on high, and behold who hath created these things, that bringeth out their host by number: He calleth them all by names by the greatness of His might, for that He is strong in power; not one faileth." Isa. 40:26. This will be one of the *texts*: and the brilliant galaxy of the heavens, with its suns, systems, orbits, and laws, and the literature of the subject, will be the *study*-book. And as the student contemplates the innumerable host, and remembers that God not only knows the collective number of them all, but brings out each one by its own number; that He calls each one by its particular name, and never forgets—not one ever slips His mind or escapes His attention—either its number or its name; and that by this infinite knowledge and this attention that touches the infinitesimal, each one is kept exactly in its orbit and in its time to a spider's web space in ages upon ages—as thus he learns in the study-book and there falls upon his ear the pleading inquiry of the next verse in the Textbook, "Why sayest thou,...My way is hid from the Lord, and My judgment is passed over from My God?" he *knows* that He who calls these all by their names, and *thinks upon him*, will never forget his name, nor shall he ever fail of the infinite attention.

Another text may be, "Canst thou bind the sweet influences of Pleiades?" Job 38:31. With that as a *text*, all the astronomy of the Pleiades will be the *study-book*. And when the student has covered the field of the Pleiades, and knows what *are* the sweet attractive influences of the Pleiades, he will know that he can know, in his own life, the sweet influences of the Spirit of Him who gave sweet influences to the Pleiades; and that will make him in *his place* in the order of God what the Pleiades are in their place in the order of God.

He can read also the *text*, "He healeth the broken in heart, and bindeth up their wounds. He telleth the number of the stars; He calleth them all by their names." Ps. 147:3, 4. And when he has studied the look of the Pleiades and their sweet influences, and Orion and his bands, and knows that He can "bind the sweet influences of the Pleiades, and loose the bands of Orion," he will also know that He can bind up the broken heart and heal the wounded spirit, and loose the bands of sin and evil habits that hold his soul in bondage. He will then be better able to appreciate, and more ready to accept, the call to "Seek Him that maketh the seven stars [the Pleiades] and Orion." Amos 5:8.

PHYSICAL GEOGRAPHY

Physical geography of the sea, as well as of the land, will be a study in all Christian schools: that is the science of the winds and the waves, the atmosphere, the rain, the dew, the ocean tides, the ocean itself. One of the *texts* may be: "The wind goeth toward the south, and turneth about unto the north; it whirleth about continually, and the wind returneth again according to his circuits." Eccl. 1:6. With that as the *text*, the teacher will lead the students into the *study-book* of the course of the winds as they come out of the north, as they go toward the south, as they whirl about continually, and as they return again according to their circuits. He will lead the students into the books that give the science of the winds, and so will conduct the students

The Study of Physical Science—*Continued*.

along the course of the circuit of the winds. Then the students will know that the wind has a circuit as certainly as the sun a course, and that the gentlest breeze that fans the cheek on a summer's day is wafted by the hand of Him who "causeth His wind to blow," and "maketh the winds His messengers."

Another text may be: "All the rivers run into the sea; yet the sea is not full; unto the place from whence the rives come, thither they return again." Eccl. 1:7. That will be the *text*: the *study-book* will be whatsoever in the science, the philosophy, and the literature of the subject will give to the student the actual facts, the procedure, and the means by which God, in calling "for the waters of the sea, and" pouring "them out upon the face of the earth" (Amos 5:8), picks up the water from the sea, transports it over the earth, and pours it out again—two hundred and fifty-five cubic *miles* of water every twenty-four hours: how "He causeth the vapors to ascend from the ends of the earth," till "by watering He wearieth the thick cloud," and then "maketh lightnings" to pierce the thick cloud "for the rain," causing "it to come, whether for correction, or for His land, or for mercy."

As thus there is studied how God "calleth for the waters of the sea" that He may pour "them out on the face of the earth," the sea itself will be found a wonderful study-book. Why is it that the waters that are called from the sea and poured out upon the face of the earth are perfectly fresh, while the waters of the sea are extremely salt? *Why is the sea salt?* What wonderful and vital consequences flow from the fact that in the beginning God made the sea salt instead of fresh? How is it that the greatest rivers of the world, and of water as warm as 86 degrees Fahrenheit, are in the oceans, one in the Atlantic and one in the Pacific: the one making the soft and beautiful climate of the British Isles, and the other that of the North Pacific Coast of America, while both these regions are in the latitude of bleak and frozen

Labrador. How is it that by this mighty river in the Atlantic alone, there is transported and discharged *perpetually* a quantity of heat "sufficient to raise mountains of iron from zero to the melting point, and to keep in flow from them a molten stream of metal greater in volume than the waters daily discharged from the Mississippi River"? How is it that in God's calling for the waters of the sea, and pouring them out upon the face of the earth *in the form of snow*, in producing a quantity of those fragile crystals that a child might easily hold in his hands, there is exerted power sufficient to pick up one of the mightiest of Alpine stone avalanches and toss it to twice the height whence it started?

"In the pursuit of this subject, the mind is led from nature up to the Great Architect of nature; and what mind will the study of this subject not fill with profitable emotions? Harmonious in their action, the air and sea are obedient to law and subject to order in all their movements. When we consult them in the performance of their manifold and marvelous offices, they teach us lessons concerning the wonders of the deep, the mysteries of the sky, the greatness, and the wisdom, and the goodness of the Creator, which makes us wiser and better men. The investigations into the broad spreading circle of phenomena connected with the winds of heaven and the waves of the sea are second to none for the good which they do and the lessons which they teach. The astronomer is said to see the hand of God in the sky; but does not the right-minded mariner, who looks aloft as he ponders over these things, hear His voice in every wave that 'claps its hands,' and feel His presence in every wind that blows? Unchanged and unchanging alone, of all created things, the ocean is the great emblem of its everlasting Creator. 'He treadeth upon the waves of the sea,' and is seen in the wonders of the deep." "The seas lift up their voice," "the waves clap their hands," at the presence of the Lord; and "deep calleth unto deep at the noise of Thy waterspouts;" for

The Study of Physical Science—*Continued*.

"The Lord hath His way in the whirlwind and in the storm, and the clouds are the dust of His feet."

BOTANY

Botany must be studied in Christian schools everywhere: however, as already observed, not botany as the term is commonly understood, as a "science" in which the flowers are considered only under an unpronounceable name, in a foreign language, and are torn to pieces to be studied, and each part given another such name. Not that, but the flowers themselves *as they are* as made by God, and as they grow, as an expression of the thought of God. One of the texts may be: "Consider the lilies of the field, how they grow." Then, the *lily itself*, and how it grows—with all the history, the literature, and the science of the lily—will be the *study-book*. That will be the field of study on that *text*. And for what purpose? Why does Jesus tell us to "consider the lilies of the field, how they grow;" that is, to *study* the lily?—For the reason stated in that other place where it is written: "Israel...shall grow as the lily." Christians, even the students themselves, are to grow, under God, as the lily grows. Jesus tells every student to study the lily, to see and know how it grows, so that he may know how he himself is to grow. He is to find in the lily the life and the power of God by which it grows,—the means which God employs in the sunshine, the soil, the dew, and the rain, to cause it to grow,—and the science and philosophy of the growing itself, so that he may know how God will cause him *himself* to "grow as the lily." Then, every student studying botany that way, only so far as the lily is concerned, will, whenever he sees a lily, get from that lily a lesson direct from God, telling him what God is doing in *his* life, and what God will put into his life by his believing on Him.

Another text may be: He "shall revive as the corn, and grow as the vine." That is the *text*; and the *study-book* will be

The Place of the Bible in Education

the *corn* and the *vine* themselves, in all the science, the philosophy, the literature, and the Scripture that can be found relating to the nature of the corn and the vine. "Except a corn of wheat fall into the ground and die, it abideth alone: but if it die, it bringeth forth much fruit." "I am the true Vine, and My Father is the Husbandman." "Ye are the branches." Thus the corn and the vine will be the *study-book* for the student who has in the Bible the *text*, Israel "shall revive as the corn, and grow as the vine." Then whenever he sees either corn or vine anywhere, it will speak to him lessons of instruction and experience, in the language of God.

Another thing: It is impossible to "consider" the flowers, the corn, the vine, the trees, "how they grow," without considering them as they grow *where they are growing*. This takes the student into the garden, the fields, the woods, where by every faculty of his being he can be receiving instruction from the great Teacher. And thus, instead of as a sluggard sitting in a house and studying the dead and dried-up forms of ants, butterflies, and other creeping or flying things which some "scientist" has caught and cruelly impaled alive, teachers and students will be in harmony with the instruction of the divine Teacher: "*Go to the ant, thou sluggard*." Do not sit and wait lazily for some "scientist" or hired boy to catch the ant and bring it dead to you; do not even be so indolent as to be content with sitting in the house and reading what has been written by some live and sensible person who *did* "go to the ant." No: go yourself. "Go to the ant, thou sluggard; consider her ways"—not consider especially her*self*, but "consider her *ways*"—"and be *wise*." And this which is thus learned from the flowers and trees, from the beasts, the birds, and creeping things, is a deeper knowledge than can be learned from printed books. Collect all the words and shades of meaning in our language on a subject, and yet all this will fall far short of expressing the fulness of thought that is conveyed to the

The Study of Physical Science—*Continued*.

mind and heart when, for instance, the delicate and demure little violet speaks in its own native and divine language to one who understands.

NATURAL PHILOSOPHY

From any part of creation there are open doors inviting the open-eyed student into every other part. An exceedingly pleasing one of these is from botany to natural philosophy. There are flowers which produce no seed, but grow only from the roots of their kind. There are flowers also which have their seeds in themselves after their kind. Of this latter kind is the innocent and chaste snowdrop. "Botanists tell us that the constitution of this plant is such as to require that, at a certain stage of its growth, the stalk should bow its head, that an operation may take place which is necessary in order that the herb should produce seed after its kind; and that; after this fecundation, its *vegetable health* requires that it should lift its head again and stand erect." And in this delicate balancing of that little flower there is wrapped up the *philosophy of gravitation*, which is simply the balancing of the universe. For "if the mass of the earth had been greater or less [than it is], the force of gravity would have been different; in that case the strength of fiber in the snowdrop, as it is, would have been too much or too little; the plant could not bow or raise its head at the right time; fecundation could not take place; and its family would have become extinct with the first individual that was planted, because its 'seed' would not have been 'in itself,' and therefore it could not have reproduced itself, and its creation would have been a failure."

Therefore, "philosophy teaches us that, when was created the little snowdrop which in our garden walks we see raising its beautiful head, at 'the singing of birds,' to remind us that 'the winter is over and gone,' the whole mass of the earth, from pole to pole, and from

The Place of the Bible in Education

circumference to center, must have been taken into account and weighed, in order that the proper degree of strength might be given to its tiny fibers." And one of the Scripture texts that tell this philosophical truth is Isa. 40:12: "Who hath *measured the waters* in the hollow of His hand, and *meted out heaven* with the span, and *comprehended the dust* of the earth in a *measure*, and *weighed* the mountains in *scales*, and *the hills* in a *balance*?" The hills are balanced with the mountains, the mountains with the earth, the earth with the waters, with the air, and also with the tiny flower that grows from its bosom, and all with the grand universe throughout.

> "God made the earth, the air, and the water; and the whole arrangement of the animal and vegetable kingdoms; just as they are and in exact counterpoise. If it were not so, why was power given to the winds to lift up and transport moisture, and to feed the plants with nourishment? or why was the property given to the sea by which its waters may become vapor, and then fruitful showers or gentle dews? If the proportions and properties of land, sea, and air were not adjusted according to the reciprocal capacities of all to perform the functions required by each, why should we be told that He 'measured the waters in the hollow of His hand, and meted out heaven with a span, and comprehended the dust of the earth in a measure, and weighed the mountains in scales, and the hills in a balance'? Why did He mete 'out the heaven with the span,' but that He might mete out the atmosphere in exact proportion to all the rest, and impart to it those properties and powers which it was necessary for it to have, in order that it might perform all those offices and duties for which He designed it?
>
> "In contemplating the system of terrestrial adaptations, these researches teach one to regard the mountain ranges and the great deserts of the earth as the astronomer does the counterpoises to his telescope—though they be mere dead weights, they

The Study of Physical Science—*Continued*.

are, nevertheless, necessary to make the balance complete, the adjustments of his machine perfect. These counterpoises give ease to the motions, stability to the performance, and accuracy to the workings, of the instrument. They are 'compensations.'

"Whenever I turn to contemplate the works of nature, I am struck with the admirable system of compensation, with the beauty and nicety with which every department is poised by the others: things and principles are meted out in directions apparently the most opposite, but in proportions so exactly balanced and nicely adjusted that results the most harmonious are produced. It is by the action of opposite and compensating forces that the earth is kept in its orbit, and the stars are held suspended in the azure vault of heaven. And these forces are so exquisitely adjusted that, at the end of a thousand years, the earth, the sun, the moon, and every star in the firmament, is found to come and stand in its proper place at the proper moment."

This law or system of compensations is called gravitation. The word "gravitation" is derived from the word *gravus*, signifying "weight." The *law of gravitation* is the law by which each particle of matter in the universe draws with its full weight upon, attracts, or is balanced with, every other particle. Another Scripture text that tells this truth of natural philosophy, and also defines what gravitation is, is Heb. 1:1–3: "God, who at sundry times and in divers manners spake in time past unto the fathers by the prophets, hath in these last days spoken unto us by His Son, whom He hath appointed heir of all things, by whom also He made the worlds; who being the brightness of His glory, and the express image of His person, and *upholding all things by the word of His power*."

This "power" of the creative and mighty Word of God is the true definition of gravitation. For gravitation is that by which all things are balanced and held in place: that by which all things are held up. Yet in the field of accepted science alone, that is as far as a student is generally allowed to go. He may ask, What holds all things up? The answer is, Gravitation. He may then ask, What is gravitation? The answer usually is, That which holds all things up: or its equivalent. But that is not a valid answer: it is only asking him to move in a circle, and find no goal. Now, in a Christian school, when it is taught that the law, or system of balances, according to which all things are held up and in their relative places, is gravitation; and then the earnest student honestly asks, But what is gravitation itself? the answer is, The present, immanent power of the living Word of God. In Christian education no student is ever left in a maze, nor is he asked to move in a circle. He is taught to the limit, and caused to stand face to face with God, in whom mind and heart find rest and satisfaction as the Fountain of knowledge.

Chapter 20.

Literature, History, Law, Logic.

THE English language and English literature must be studied in Christian schools: "Our own tongue, second to that of Greece alone in force and copiousness:" "our own literature, second to none that ever existed." And in this field, as in every other proper one, the Bible stands preeminent.

As to the language, the English of the Bible is the purest and best English that there is in the world. There are in the Bible more pure English words, and better English words, than in any other book in the English language. Then, whoever would become acquainted with the purest and best English *must* study the English of the Bible.

In the English of the Bible there is more said in fewer words than in any other writing in the world. This directness and forcefulness, this true weightiness, is the characteristic of the language of the Bible above that of all other writings. And the person whose vocabulary is composed most fully of the words, the phraseology, and the forthrightness of the Bible, will be the most direct and forcible speaker or writer, will be able to say most in fewest words.

The Bible holds such an immense advantage over all other matter in English that to it it belongs by true merit to be the beginning of all study in English literature, and the basis and guide of all study of English literature in other books. Yet this is not all. To say that the Bible is deservedly the beginning, basis, and guide in the study of English literature is not enough. The Bible in itself alone is a whole

The Place of the Bible in Education

English Literature. This truth has been best expressed by Macaulay, in his allusion to the Bible as "that stupendous work, the English Bible—a Book which, if everything else in our language should perish, would alone suffice to show the whole extent of its beauty and power."—*Essay on Dryden.* No one who is acquainted with the English Bible, and the spirit of it, and with other literature in English, will question for a moment this estimate of the wealth of the Bible as English Literature. In the Bible there is every phase of literature that is involved in the art of human expression, or in the portrayal of human feeling. And the transcendent merit of the Bible in all this is that it is all true. Its scenes are all adopted from real life, and are drawn to the life. They are not "founded on fact:" they *are* fact.

On the other hand, how much of that which is studied today as English literature, in the schools, colleges, and universities, is true? Is not nine-tenths of it fiction? And is it not the fictional that stands the highest in these schools, as literature? What can give a man prominence today in the world of English literature more quickly than the writing of a popular novel? Even a minister of the gospel, an earnest, godly, powerful minister of the gospel, never can gain the prominence, even among people who profess the gospel, by simply preaching the gospel of the Word of God, that he is assured of by the writing of a popular novel: and especially if he writes two or three, and so demonstrates that he has special ability as a novelist. That is to say, his standing as a minister of the Word of God, which is truth, is made to be dependent on his popularity as a producer of fiction![6]

---

[6] Another notable and pernicious defect in the study of English literature is that from its true plane it has degenerated to the study and exaltation of *the man who wrote it.* This would be a total missing of the true aim in the study of literature, when the men who are studied and exalted are worthy of such notice; but in many cases these men are utterly unworthy to be brought to the attention of youth in any such connection.

Literature, History, Law, Logic.

Now which is better, which is the more Christian for Christians, or for a Christian school—to study English literature that is inferior in quality, and is fictional besides, or to study it in that "Book which, if everything else in our language should perish, would alone suffice to show the whole extent of its beauty and power," and which, in addition, is all the very perfection of truth—the truth of God! To ask the question is certainly only to answer it, in the mind of every Christian and in the mind of every person who would receive a Christian education.

When this can all truly be said of the Bible as compared with the literature of Christendom, what shall not be said of it in contrast to the literature of paganism?

> "It has come to be generally recognized that the classics of Greece and Rome stand to us in the position of an ancestral literature,—the inspiration of our great masters, and bond of common association between our poets and their readers. But does not such a position belong equally to the literature of the Bible? If our intellect and imagination have been formed by the Greeks, have we not in similar fashion drawn our moral and emotional training from Hebrew thought? Whence, then, the neglect of the Bible in our higher schools and colleges?
>
> "It is one of the curiosities of our civilization that we are content to go for our liberal education to literatures which, morally, are at an opposite pole from ourselves: literatures in which the most exalted tone is often an apotheosis of the sensuous, which degrade divinity, not only to the human level, but to the lowest level of humanity. Our hardest social problem being temperance, we study in Greek the glorification of intoxication. While in mature life we are occupied in tracing law to the remotest corner of the universe, we go at school for literary impulse to the poetry that dramatizes the burden of hopeless fate. Our highest politics aim at conserving the arts of peace; our first poetic lessons are in an *Iliad* that can not be

The Place of the Bible in Education

appreciated without a bloodthirsty joy in killing. We seek to form a character in which delicacy and reserve shall be supreme, and at the same time are training our taste in literatures which, if published as English books, would be seized by the police.

"I recall these paradoxes, not to make objection, but to suggest the reasonableness of the claim that the one side of our liberal education should have another side to balance it. Prudish fears may be unwise, but there is no need to put an embargo upon decency. It is surely good that our youth, during the formative period, should have displayed to them, in a literary dress as brilliant as that of Greek literature—in lyrics which Pindar can not surpass, in rhetoric as forcible as that of Demosthenes, or contemplative prose not inferior to Plato's—a people dominated by an utter passion for righteousness, a people whom ideas of purity, of infinite good, of universal order, of faith in the irresistible downfall of all moral evil, moved to a poetic passion as fervid, and speech as musical, as when Sappho sang of love or Æschylus thundered his deep notes of destiny."[7]

It has been truly said of the book of Isaiah alone, that "It may be safely asserted that nowhere else in the literature of the world have so many colossally great ideas been brought together within the limits of a single work." This can be extended to include the whole Bible, and it still be equally true.

So also the following:

"Even in literary form the world has produced nothing greater than Isaiah; and the very difficulty of determining its literary form is so much evidence how cramped and imperfect literary criticism has been made by the confinement of its outlook to the single type of literature which has come to monopolize the

---

[7] Richard G. Moulton, professor of Literature in English in Chicago University, *The Literary Study of the Bible* preface, p. xii.

Literature, History, Law, Logic.

name 'classical.' But when we proceed to the matter and thought of Isaiah—the literary matter, quite apart from the theology founded on it—how can we explain the neglect of such a masterpiece in our plans of liberal education?

"It is the boast of England and America that their higher education is religious in its spirit. Why is it, then, that our youth are taught to associate exquisiteness of expression, force of presentation, brilliance of imaginative picturing, only with literatures in which the prevailing matter and thought are on a low moral plane? Such a paradox is part of *the paganism which came in with the Renaissance*, and which our higher education is still too conservative to shake off."[8]

Shall it be that *Christians* in their education will still refuse to shake off this paganism? Shall not the supreme Christian literature—the Bible—have its own supreme place alone at every stage and in every phase of Christian education?

HISTORY.

History, both national and church, as separate, as related and as interrelated, is an essential study in all Christian schools. And for the study of universal history, of national history, and of church history, from the Flood until now, and to the end of the world, the Bible is the one grand text-book, the Book of fundamental and sure-guiding principles. There alone are given the origin and distribution of the race. There alone are given the origin and causes of history. There alone are given the origin and causes of civil government, of the state, of monarchy, of empire.

---

8   *Modern Reader's Bible*, Isaiah, preface. p. xxiv.

The Place of the Bible in Education

"The God of nature has written His existence in all His works, and His law in the heart of man." He has written His character in the Bible and His providence amongst the nations. He "hath made of one blood all nations of men for to dwell on all the face of the earth, and hath determined the times before appointed, and the bounds of their habitation;" "He divided to the nations their inheritance;" "that they should seek the Lord, if haply they might feel after Him, and find Him, though He be not far from every one of us." "God hath spoken once; twice have I heard this; that power belongeth unto God." "There is no power but of God: the powers that be are ordained of God." "He is the Governor among the nations." "The Most High ruleth in the kingdom of men, and giveth it to whomsoever He will." "He removeth kings, and setteth up kings;" "calling from a far country the man that executeth His counsel."

"History, therefore, with its dusty and moldering pages, is to us as sacred a volume as the book of nature;" for history properly studied is but the study of the progress of the grand purposes of God through all the vicissitudes of man and the nations. History thus studied is found to be far more than a record of marches, battles, and sieges in the rise and fall of nations: far more than the story of the Nimrods, the Pharaohs, the Alexanders, Caesars, and Napoleons. All these events and persons will to be found to be but incidents in the far greater story of the *significance* of events, and of the real meaning of the life of man and nations on the earth: only incidental to the grand philosophy of things that is over all and through all and in all. "History" has been aptly defined as "philosophy teaching by example." But upon this as upon other subjects the important question is, *What philosophy?* Shall it be a human philosophy conjured up and read into the "example," or extracted from the example? or shall it be the divine philosophy revealed and preceding all, and so being really *philosophy teaching*, and philosophy *really teaching*, by

Literature, History, Law, Logic.

example? In the Bible alone is found the philosophy of universal history.

In history as in other studies the Bible supplies the text, stating the *principle*, the leading fact, or a symbolical description, each of which contains a volume: this for the text and guide, then all that can be found in the Bible, in native inscriptions, or in any other writings on that subject, will be the study-book. The Bible, as it stands from Genesis to the captivity to Babylon, is the true text-book of the history, both national and church, of that period. From the captivity to Babylon to the end of the world, that portion of the Bible from the captivity to Babylon unto the end *of the Book* is the text-book of the whole history, both national and church. And in this portion of the Bible the books of Daniel and Revelation are the keys: Daniel especially to national history, and Revelation especially to church history.

When once this secret of history is found, he who finds it will be surprised to find how much of the history of the world there is in the Bible alone. Instances will be found in which, with the exception of dates and individual names, the whole history of a nation is told in from one to half a dozen verses in the Bible. Take, for instance, Dan. 7:4: "The first was like a lion, and had eagle's wings: I beheld till the wings thereof were plucked, and it was lifted up from the earth, and made stand upon the feet as a man, and a man's heart was given to it." That one verse tells the whole history of the Babylonian Empire. And when all that has been elsewhere written on that subject has been read, it will be found that, though more specific facts and details and the names of men are told, *not* more of *the truth* of the story is told than is couched in the symbolism of that one verse. Indeed it will be found that all that is elsewhere written of the history of the Babylonian Empire is truly but the filling in of the expressive outline thus drawn. There are in the Bible enough other such instances to make a book; but this is sufficient to illustrate the principle of the Bible as the text-book and guide in the study of history.

LAW.

Law is a subject that must be studied in Christian schools; and the Bible must be the only text-book—not law as the term is used and generally understood by lawyers and judges in earthly courts; but as the term is used and understood by the Judge in the Court of heaven—law as it is in the divine principles of justice and righteousness: law as it is involved in the guilt and the justification, the sin and the forgiveness, of man.

This study is also essential for the instruction of youth in the principles of daily conduct. It is painful to see the indifference of professed Christians to the principles of daily justice and righteousness between man and man as they are made perfectly plain in the Scriptures, especially in the books of Exodus, Leviticus, and Deuteronomy.

The truth is that every Christian should read, over and over, simply for the principles of daily justice and fair and honest dealing, Exodus 20–24; Leviticus 19, 25; and the book of Deuteronomy; until these principles become his very life; then read and reread the sermon on the mount, and the first eight, and from the twelfth to the fourteenth, chapters of Romans. All this as the study of law as such, in the fundamental principles of law that must be manifested in the conduct of the daily affairs of Christian life and Christian business. Every Christian, and especially every Christian who occupies any position of responsibility or trust in institutions or business of either God or men, should read over and over these portions of Scripture. These principles faithfully inculcated upon the minds and graven upon the hearts of youth in school, will be worth a thousand times more both to them and to the world than can be all the human law in the world.

Literature, History, Law, Logic.

LOGIC.

Logic must be studied in Christian schools. And the Bible must be the only text-book; not the logic of Aristotle, or of any other man; not the formal logic that is in the books; but the logic is manifested in the divine reasoning that is in the Bible. That is, the Word of God must be studied until the very thoughts in that Word shall become the thoughts of the one who studies; until the reasoning, the logic, of the Word of God shall be his reasoning; yea, till the very mind that gave the Word of God shall become his mind.

This only is Christian logic. And only such study as this is the study of Christian logic. In this the Bible is not only the text-book, but also the study-book. For is it possible to find truer logic, sounder reasoning, than in the divine reasoning? And has not the Author of reason extended the invitation to all people, "Come now, and let us *reason* TOGETHER"? What more blessed invitation, what higher honor, what grander prospect, than this could ever be placed before a reasoning mind?

However, the time would fail us to take up every subject within the field of true knowledge and education; we can not exhaust the Bible as the true educational book. But it is earnestly hoped that what has in these pages been presented may awaken attention, and turn the allegiance of Christians to the Bible in its true place in education. For it is literally true that there is nothing in the world that can create mental capacity and give intellectual power as will the study of the Word of God as pleaded for in this book.

One of the defenses that is offered in behalf of the study of the pagan "classics" in the face of their essential immorality, is that "the idea is not that the student shall gather the philosophy, or the instruction, that is in this

The Place of the Bible in Education

literature; but it is used primarily *as the best means of developing the mind*, of creating mental vigor, of increasing intellectual power." For the occasion let the validity of this plea be admitted. A student is conducted through that course unto its completion. Suppose the impossible, that he has been successful in excluding from his mind the immoral substance of the matter studied; and has attained the full benefit of its power to create capacity. What must be the result?—A superior capacity; *but what is in it?* He has the capacity, if you will; but as for any real good, it is *empty*. And let nobody ever forget that with mankind as it is in this world, and especially in these days, every degree of capacity that is ever created and *not filled with that which is good*, will inevitably be occupied with that which is *not* good. And therein lies the perniciousness of the proposition that the years of the most receptive and formative period in the lives of youth can be largely spent in literatures that are essentially immoral, and yet the immorality that is in the very substance of the literature find no place in their minds! That can no more be so than that they can carry fire in their bosoms and they not be burned, or handle pitch and they not be defiled.

The true philosophy of education is to develop capacity only with the good; and to develop it no faster than can it be filled with the good, the useful, and the practical. Let Christians hold only to the education that will put into the mind only that which is good, true, useful, and practical. The Bible as the basis of all education and the text-book in every line of study, will assure this. The philosophy of it is this: Christian education, true education, is of faith. Faith comes by the Word of God. As this faith which comes by the Word of God is exercised in the Word of God and upon the Word of God, it "groweth exceedingly," and thus develops capacity on its own part. On the other side, the righteousness of God is revealed to each degree of the exercise and development of faith; "from faith to faith."

Literature, History, Law, Logic.

And the righteousness of God is an *expanding principle*. Thus capacity is developed also from that side. And so the capacity being developed from the side of the individual by the exercise and exceeding growth of faith, and from the side of God by the expanding power of the righteousness of God revealed to each degree of exceedingly growing faith; *with no degree of capacity developed that is not filled to the full with the supremely good and true;* and this all accomplished through the Word of God; the Bible thus stands as the greatest educating power in the world. And the Scripture text that expresses the principle is Col. 1:9, 10: I cease not "to pray for you, and to desire that ye might *be filled* with the knowledge of His will in all wisdom and spiritual understanding; that ye might walk worthy of the Lord unto all pleasing, being fruitful in every good work, *and increasing* in the knowledge of God." "Filled" and yet "increasing:" ever "filled" and ever "increasing," unto the being "filled with all the fulness of God." Thus the Bible as the basis of all education has the true philosophy in it.

Christian education is more than the cultivation of the intellectual part of man: it is the cultivation of the moral as supreme, and the highest possible cultivation of the intellectual only as tributary to the supremely moral. Yet neither is it the cultivation of only the intellectual and the moral: it is also the cultivation of the physical as well. And this, too, as tributary to both the intellectual and the moral. Morality is the only security in education. And Christianity is the only true morality. Christian education, therefore, is the symmetrical and the highest possible cultivation of every faculty,—physical, intellectual, and moral,—in order to glorify God on the earth, and finish the work that He has given Christians to do.

One day the writer and a graduate of a prominent university, who was at the time also the editor of a leading magazine in the United States, were talking together of the principles and view of education that are now presented in this book. When the principle of it was clearly caught, the university graduate and editor exclaimed: "Why, with such a system as that in full operation, every one of your schools will be a university; and every teacher will be a genius—he will *have* to be."

It is true. When Christians truly get God's view of education, and carry it out in the Spirit and power of God, it is true that every Christian school will be a university. It will not be *called* that, for those Christians will hold modest views of their abilities and attainments; but it will be that. With the universal Book as the text-book; with the universe itself as the study-book; with the universal Teacher as the Head of each school; and with teachers who are guided and taught by the universal Spirit; what but true universities can such schools be? The greatest consideration in it all is that in this way the student is always living and thinking and walking and working with God. And that alone is a university.

Chapter 21.

The Failures of Popular Education.

SERIOUS complaint is made and for years has been made of the failures of the whole system of education as conducted, from the primary grades to the university and the theological seminary. These complaints are not made by mere carping critics, but by the leading and most responsible educators of the whole country. One of the leading magazines—the *Cosmopolitan*—published a series of articles extending through a whole year, pointing out the serious defects in the system, under the significant inquiry, "Does a College Education Educate?" The articles were written by acknowledged masters in education. The *Outlook*, one of the leading religious weeklies of the country, has had much to say in the same direction. The *Ladies' Home Journal*, in the delightfully plain and winning style of its editor, has not spared to declare whole and wholesome counsel in the matter. President Eliot, of Harvard University, one of the leading educators not only of the United States, but of the world, being in position to speak with authority on the subject, has done so in no uncertain terms: in set addresses to educators pointing out that "the shortcomings and failures in American education, and the disappointments concerning its results, have been many and grievous." Even the United States Senate was obliged to take cognizance of this subject; and with disappointing results.

The Place of the Bible in Education

A few illustrative extracts are here presented. At the annual meeting of the Connecticut State Teachers' Association in New Haven, Oct. 17, 1902, President Eliot, of Harvard, delivered an address "advocating the expenditure of more money for education in the United States on the ground that the shortcomings and failures in American education have been many and grievous." The following is a summary in his own words of the evidences of the failure of popular education:—

> 1. *Drunkenness.*—"For more than two generations we have been struggling with the barbarous vice of drunkenness, but have not yet discovered a successful method of dealing with it. The legislation of the states has been variable and in moral significance uncertain.
>
> "In some of the states of the Union we have been depending on prohibitory legislation, but the intelligence of the people has been insufficient either to enforce such legislation or to substitute better."
>
> 2. *Gambling.*—"The persistence of gambling in the United States is another disappointing thing to the advocates of popular education, for gambling is an extraordinarily unintelligent form of pleasurable excitement. It is a prevalent vice among all savage people, but one which a moderate cultivation of the intelligence, a very little foresight, and the least sense of responsibility should be sufficient to eradicate."
>
> 3. *Bad Government.*—"It must be confessed that the results of universal suffrage are not in all respects what we should have expected from a people supposed to be prepared at school for an intelligent exercise of suffrage. We have discovered from actual observation that universal suffrage often produces bad government, especially in large cities."
>
> 4. *Crime, Mob, and Riot.*—"It is a reproach to popular education that the gravest crimes of violence are committed in great number all over the United States, in the older states as well as in the new, by individuals and by mobs, and with a large measure of

The Failures of Popular Education.

impunity. The population produces a considerable number of burglars, robbers, rioters, lynchers, and murderers, and is not intelligent enough either to suppress or to exterminate these criminals."

5. *Bad Reading.*—"The nature of the daily reading supplied to the American public affords much ground for discouragement." "Since one invaluable result of education is a taste for good reading, the purchase by the people of thousands of tons of ephemeral reading matter, which is not good in either form or substance, shows that one great end of popular education has not been attained."

6. *The Popular Theater.*—"The popular taste is for trivial spectacles, burlesque, vulgar vaudeville, extravaganza, and melodrama, and the stage often presents to unmoved audiences scenes and situations of an unwholesome sort.."

7. *Medical Delusions.*—"Americans…are the greatest consumers of patent medicines in the known world, and the most credulous patrons of all sorts of 'medicine men' and women, and of novel healing arts."

8. *Labor Strikes.*—"That labor strikes should occur more and more frequently, and be more and more widespread, has been another serious disappointment in regard to the outcome of popular education. As we have all seen lately, the strike is often resorted to for reasons not made public, or, at least, not made public until after the strike has taken place."

On "the educational processes of our time"—the prevailing "skeptical, analytical, critical process of inquiry and investigation;" the process in which "Doubt is the pedagogue which leads the pupil to knowledge;" the *Outlook*, April 21, 1900, remarks:—

"Does he study the human body?—Dissection and anatomy are the foundations of his study.

"Chemistry?—The laboratory furnishes him the means of analysis and inquiry into physical substances.

The Place of the Bible in Education

"History?—He questions the statements which have been unquestioned heretofore, ransacks libraries for authorities in ancient volumes and more ancient documents.

"Literature?—The poem which he read only to enjoy he now subjects to the scalpel, inquires whether it really is beautiful, why it is beautiful, how its meter should be classified, how its figures have been constructed.

"Philosophy?—He subjects his own consciousness to a process of vivisection in an endeavor to ascertain the physiology and anatomy of the human spirit, brings his should into the laboratory that he may learn its chemical constituents.

"Meanwhile the *constructive* and synthetic process is relegated to a second place, or lost sight of altogether.

"Does he study *medicine*?—He gives more attention to diagnosis than to therapeutics, to the analysis of disease than to the problem how to overcome it.

"Law?—He spends more time in analyzing cases than in developing power to grasp great principles and apply them in the administration of justice to varying conditions.

"The classics?—It is strange if he has not at graduation spent more *weeks* in the syntax and grammar of the language than he has spent *hours* in acquiring and appreciating the thought and the spirit of the great classic authors. It has been well and truly said of the modern student that he does not study, grammar to understand Homer, he reads Homer to get the Greek grammar.

"His historical study has given him dates, events, a mental historical chart; perhaps, too, it has given him a scholar's power to discriminate between the true and the false, the historical and the mythical in ancient legends; but *not to many* has it given an understanding of the *significance of events*, a comprehension of, or even any new light upon the real meaning of the life of man on the earth.

The Failures of Popular Education.

"Has he been studying philosophy?—Happy is he if, as a result of his analysis of self-consciousness, he has not become morbid respecting his own inner life, or cynically skeptical concerning the inner life of others.

"It is doubtless in the realm of ethics and religion that the *disastrous results* of a too exclusive analytical process and a too exclusive critical spirit are seen.

"Carrying the *same spirit*, applying the *same methods*, to the *investigation of religion*, the Bible becomes to him simply a collection of ancient literature, whose sources, structure, and forms he studies, *whose spirit he*, at least for the time, *forgets*; *worship* is *a ritual* whose origin, rise, and development he investigates; whose *real significance* as an expression of penitence, gratitude, and consecration *he loses sight of altogether*. *Faith* is a series of *tenets* whose biological development he traces; or a form of consciousness whose relation to brain action he inquires into; or whose growth by evolutionary processes out of earlier states he endeavors to retrace: forgetting meanwhile what is the meaning of the *experience itself* as *a present fact* in human life, what vital force and significance it possesses:

"Vivisection is almost sure sooner or later to become a post-mortem; and the subject of it, whether it be a flower, a body, an author, or an experience, generally dies under the scalpel. It is *for this reason* that so many students in school, academy, and college *lose*, not merely their theology, which is perhaps no great loss, but *their religion*, which is an irreparable loss, while they are acquiring an education."

The city of Washington is credited with having the best schools and the best school system in the United States. But there came to the United States Senate Committee on District of Columbia so many complaints concerning the work done in those schools that the Senate appointed a committee to investigate the whole subject. What this committee found will be suggested by the following notice of their report to the Senate, published in the literary

The Place of the Bible in Education

supplement of the *New York Times*, June 23, 1900, under the heading "Queer School Work":—

"There was an investigation to find about what was the condition of the pupils on their entrance into the high schools at the average age of fourteen. At that point they had had all the schooling they were expected to get in arithmetic; they had been studying the history of their country for five years; and they were, in the words of the trustees, believed to be 'able to dispose correctly of almost any English sentence.' Practically they had reached the limit of the advantages that the great body of the children in any large city can get from the public schools, and were supposed to be ready for that 'higher' teaching which only a small fraction of those children can afford to take.

"It seems that in Washington the methods of teaching are supposed to be of a peculiarly advanced character, and 'the one best adapted to train the minds of children and youth, and to teach them to think and to express themselves clearly.' As early as in the fifth grade, when the children are about ten years old, emphasis is 'laid upon powers and roots, square measure, cubic measure, cube rood.' History was taught so that 'the child possessed a clear, connected, sequential view of the whole subject selected.' In the teaching of English the process is thus described:—

"The work of the fourth grade, of finding the base of the sentence, was continued, more and more difficult sentences being mastered; the idea asserted was differentiated as to identity, condition, place, time, size, etc., and action; and finally the idea was analyzed for its elements. Here the child began the study of the parts of speech, in addition to being required to know the sentence—as a whole, its parts, bases, modifiers, asserters—whether emphatic, potential, absolute, etc., and what is asserted.'

"The result of the examinations, which were framed by the Civil Service Commission, was distinctly

The Failures of Popular Education.

discouraging. In arithmetic, where *nothing was required but a knowledge of the four fundamental rules and fractions*, the pupils of only one school, some 350 out of 1,300, attained the average of 70 per cent, the lowest that would admit to the eligible list for common clerical work, while less than 30 per cent in all the schools reached that average, and only 7 per cent attained a marking of 90 per cent, which is the average of those who succeed in entering the service. As the schooling in arithmetic was *completed*, this is a bad showing.

"In history it was worse yet. Only 3.6 per cent made 90, only 19 per cent made 70, and the total average was but 53.1 per cent. One of the questions asked was as follows:—

"'Give a brief account of the Puritans, or of the Pilgrims, stating why so called, the country from which they came, their reasons for emigrating, where they settled, and some of their characteristics, habits, and customs.'

"Some of the answers throw light on the 'clear, connected, sequential view of the whole subject,' which the pupils are supposed by the fond trustees to get. For instance:—

"'Pilgrims were called pilgrims because they pilgrimed and journed.'

"'The pilgrims prayed for providence which was at times granted to them.'

"'The exiles from england were called Pilgrims after the rocky coast of Plymouth upon which they landed.'

"'The Pilgrims landed at Plymouth rock early in the spring in a small boat called the May-Flower. When they landed they were few in number. Being opposed to the weather many died. Their clothing was not very thick for winter and their shelter did not protect the cold, wind, rain, and snow from coming in.'

"These answers also give some idea of the ability acquired by the pupils to 'dispose quickly of almost any English sentence,' as do the varied modes of spelling

The Place of the Bible in Education

the names of states. Florida appears as Florda, Florido, Florada, Floridy, and floriday. Massachusetts becomes in succession Massachusettes, Massachuesettes, Masschusetts, Masschusettes, masschsuetts, Massachtusettes, and Massachewsettes.

"We have no wish to condemn the entire system of teaching in Washington from this report: it does not reveal enough about it. And we are well aware of the diabolic ingenuity of stupidity of which even well-taught children are sometimes capable; but we submit that children in the state disclosed by the facts we have cited are not fit subjects for 'higher' tuition, and that until the results of effort below the grade they have reached are very much better, the money and energy expended on that higher tuition are wasted—and worse."

When such is the record as to the educational work in the supposedly best school system in the United States, what must it be in the worst! And that this is most probably a fair showing is confirmed by the fact that, in 1900, Columbia University found itself compelled to make the common spelling-book a fixture in its curriculum, because of the barbarous inability to spell that was revealed in the matriculation papers of college graduates who applied for admission.

On the need of "a better system of education" in this country a contributor to the *Outlook*, in 1899, said: —

"There must be in this country a better system of education, a system that is in closer touch with life, and that fits rather than unfits for life. There must be something in our common schools that will make for self-respect, and for that respect for others that is a part of true self-respect; something that will develop faithfulness and intelligence and pride in work; something that will link head and hands by indissoluble bonds. Domestic science and manual training in schools will gradually give a greater respect for manual

The Failures of Popular Education.

labor; and with this respect should go a greater diffusion of manual labor; for the lack in our present system is quite as much on the side of employers as of employed.

"An intelligent and many-sided woman recently remarked to me that Queen Victoria would be a better woman if she made her own bed daily. While it may not be practicable for queens to make their own beds, or for the President of the United States to chop his own wood, there never will be faithfulness, respect, and intelligence on the side of the workers unless the same attitude toward work is found in the employers."

This same thought and the need of industrial education was emphasized in 1901 by the introduction in the House of Representatives in Congress the following:—

"A BILL

"To establish a general system of industrial education in the territories of the United States and insular dependencies.

"Be it enacted by the Senate and House of Representatives of the United States of America in Congress assembled: That there shall be established in all the territories subject to the exclusive jurisdiction of the United States, including the District of Columbia and the recently-acquired islands, a system of primary industrial education, to the end that all children may become intelligent, skillful, efficient, and self-supporting citizens.

"Section 2.—That in these schools agriculture and the ordinary arts of civilized life shall be taught practically to all youth who apply between the ages of thirteen and eighteen. Instruction shall include the sciences which underlie these arts, and every pupil shall be required to work with his hands not less than four hours daily under the direction of such schools, with adequate farms, buildings, and a competent force

The Place of the Bible in Education

of teachers, and that *such schools be free of debt*; provided further, that *all pupils shall work* with their hands for four hours daily for five days of each week of the term."

Of the need and the value of this, Prof. Edward Daniells, of Washington, D. C., wrote thus:—

"This system will cost millions, but it will soon return tenfold.

"Ignorance is the curse of the land! Not of books, but that more dangerous kind that, wrapped in the conceit of shallow culture, poses for learning and deceives the masses! The old monkish system has had its day; what was good in it has been lost in the growth of the moss and fungus of ages. The mentality of childhood is stunted, dwarfed, and smothered. In the cities it is already yielding to nature study, manual training, and some slight ameliorations. But the country youth are growing up in hopeless savagery in many states."

In urging "The Needs of American Public Education" in order to redeem it from its "many and grievous shortcomings and failures." in a public address delivered before the Rhode Island Institute of Instruction, Oct. 23, 1902, President Eliot so admirably covered the whole ground that we can do no better than to present the principal points of that address.

SCHOOLHOUSES AND GROUNDS.

He urged increased expenditure of money, and this money spent first of all in making all school buildings as nearly as possible perfectly fire-proof and sanitary. To this latter end he offered the following wise suggestion: —

The Failures of Popular Education.

"All flues, ducts, and boxes for the reception and conveyance of cold or hot air should be so built and disposed that their interiors can be cleaned. Any one who has examined with a lens the extraordinary amount of animal and vegetable matter which accumulates on a sheet of 'tangle-foot' fly-paper placed in a cold-air box, at any season of the year when the ground is not covered with snow, will heartily concur in this prescription. The observance of these rules would, of course, demand additional initial expenditure on school buildings, but would diminish the cost of maintenance."

As to the school grounds, he presented the following beautiful thought:—

"Whether in town or country, a large open space, yard, or garden should surround every school building, and should be kept with neatness and decorated with shrubs and flowers."

HEALTH OF THE PUPILS.

"Next to this improvement in schoolhouses and schoolyards comes improvement in the sanitary control and management of schools. This control requires the services of skillful physicians; and such a physician should be officially connected with every large school. It should be his duty to watch for contagious diseases, to prevent the too early return to school of children who have suffered from such diseases, to take thought for the eyes of the children lest they be injured in reading or writing by bad postures or bad light, to advise concerning the rectification of remediable bodily defects in any of the children under his supervision, to give advice at homes about the diet and sleep of the children whose nutrition is visibly defective, and, in short, to be the protector, counselor, and friend of the children and their parents with regard to

The Place of the Bible in Education

health, normal growth, and the preservation of all the senses in good condition.

"Such medical supervision of school-children would be costly, but it would be the most rewarding school expenditure that a community could make, even from the industrial or commercial point of view, since nothing impairs the well-being and productiveness of a community so much as sickness and premature disability or death. As in an individual, so in a nation, health and strength are the foundations of productiveness and prosperity."

BETTER TEACHERS.

"The next object for additional expenditure is *better teachers*. Of course, teachers should know well the subjects which they are to teach; but that is by no means sufficient. Every teacher should also know the best methods of teaching his subjects. College professors heretofore have been apt to think that knowledge of the subject to be taught was the sufficient qualification of a teacher; but all colleges, as well as all schools, have suffered immeasurable losses as a result of this delusion."

BETTER TEACHING.

"With better teachers, numerous other improvements would come in, as, for instance, a better teaching of literature and of history, and better biological and geographical instruction, these natural history studies being pursued by the pupils in the open air as well as in the school-rooms.

"I have elsewhere urged that all public open spaces, whether country parks, forests, beaches, city squares, gardens, or parkways, should be utilized for the instruction of the children of the public schools by teachers capable of interesting them in the phenomena of plant and animal life. But *this means quite a new breed of common-school teachers.*

The Failures of Popular Education.

"The teaching of geography in the open air is a delightful form of instruction; but it requires a teacher fully possessed of the principles of physiography, and knowing how to illustrate these principles on a small scale in gutters, brooks, gullies, ravines, hillsides, and hilltops.

"Some nature study of this desirable sort has been already introduced into American schools; but it is not persisted in through years enough of the school course. There is needed much more of this sort of study, beginning in the kindergarten and going through the high school."

BETTER PROGRAMS.

"An expensive improvement in the public schools, but one urgently needed, is the enrichment of the school program for the years between nine and fourteen, and the introduction of selection among studies as early as ten years of age. Unless this is done, and done soon, the public schools will cease to be resorted to by the children of well-to-do Americans. The private and endowed schools offer a choice of foreign languages, for instance, as early as ten years of age and even earlier; and everybody knows that this is the age at which to begin the study of foreign languages, whether ancient or modern. In large cities it seems to be already settled that the private and endowed schools get the children of all parents who can afford to pay their charges. One reason for this result is that the programs of the public schools are distinctly inferior to the programs of the good private and endowed schools; and they are inferior at precisely this point—they have too limited a range of studies in the years between nine and fourteen. It is, of course, not desirable that each individual child should *pursue* a great variety of studies; but it is essential that each individual child should *have access* to a variety of studies."

The Place of the Bible in Education

MANUAL TRAINING.

"In many scattered places in the United States perfect demonstration has already been given that manual training and instruction in the mechanical arts and trades are in *the first place*, valuable as means of *mental* and *moral* training, and, in the second place, useful for the individual toward obtaining a livelihood, and for the nation toward developing its industries. Accordingly, manual training schools, mechanic arts high schools and trade schools ought to become habitual parts of the American school system; and normal schools and colleges ought to provide optional instruction in these subjects, since all public school teachers ought to understand them. Such schools are more expensive than schools which do not require mechanical apparatus and the service of good mechanics as instructors; but there can be no doubt that they will repay promptly their cost to the community which maintains them."

VACATION SCHOOLS.

"Vacation schools, have also demonstrated their great usefulness in cities and large towns. The *best ones* offer *manual training* for both boys and girls, as well as book work, and are heartily welcomed by both parents and children. They combat effectively the mistaken policy of long vacations for children who can not escape from the crowded city streets and tenements. Indeed, the experience recently gained in city vacation schools and in the summer courses of colleges and universities proves that *the long summer vacation of nine to thirteen weeks is by no means necessary* to the health of either schoolchildren or maturer students. The best method is to keep the pupil in vigor *all the year* by means of frequent recesses during school hours, free half-days twice a week, and occasional respites of a week.

"Then the vacation school in summer should offer a distinct variety of work in subjects different from those

The Failures of Popular Education.

pursued the rest of the year; for children and adults alike find great refreshment in mere change of work. For example, the competent college professor may indeed seek change of air and scene during the summer vacation, but it is for the purpose of doing under advantageous conditions a kind of intellectual work different from that which engrosses him in term-time, and not with the intention of keeping his mind vacant or inert.

"Furthermore, vacation schools in the poor quarters of closely-built cities are downright refuges from the physical squalor and moral dangers of the streets. It is obvious that vacation schools on an adequate scale must cause a serious addition to school expenditure of a city or large town; for they require the services of an additional corps of teachers, and they need additional apparatus, materials, and service. It is equally obvious that these schools are urgently needed by a large proportion of the population on grounds which are simultaneously physical, mental, and moral."

THE CHURCH RECREANT.

"The church and its ministers can not be said to have risen in public estimation since the Civil War. *Its control over education has distinctly diminished.* In some of its branches it seems to cling to archaic metaphysics and morbid poetic imaginings; in others it apparently inclines to take refuge in decorums, pomps, costumes, and observances. On the whole,...it has shown little readiness to rely on the intense reality of the universal sentiments to which Jesus appealed, or to go back to the simple preaching of the gospel of brotherhood and unity—of love to God and love to man. So the church as a whole has today no influence whatever on many millions of our fellow-countrymen—called Jews or Christians, Protestants or Catholics though they be.

"We still believe that the voluntary church is the best of churches; because a religion which is accepted under compulsion is really no religion at all for the

The Place of the Bible in Education

individual soul, though it may be a social embellishment or a prop for the state. Yet, believing thus, we have to admit that the voluntary church in the United States has no hold on a large and increasing part of the population.

"By no positive fault of their own, but by a sort of negative incapacity, legislature, court, and church seem to be passing through some transition which temporarily impairs their power....To redeem and vivify legislatures, courts, and churches, what agency is so promising as education?"

THE NEED OF THE MASSES.

"We should ask ourselves what better remedy than wise popular education, what other remedy, can be imagined for the new evils which threaten society because of the new facilities for making huge combinations of producers, or middlemen; of farmers, or miners, or manufacturers; of rich or poor; of laborers or capitalists?

"Masses of men are much more excitable than average individuals, and will do in gregarious passion things which the individuals who compose the masses would not do. A crowd is dangerously liable to sudden rage or—what is worse—sudden terror, and either emotion may overpower the sense of responsibility and annihilate for the moment both prudence and mercy. There never was a time when common sentiments and desires could be so quickly massed, never a time when the force of multitudes could be so effectively concentrated at a selected point for a common purpose.

"Against this formidable danger there is only one trustworthy defense. *The masses of the people must be taught to use their reason, to seek the truth, and to love justice and mercy.* There is no safety for democratic society in, truth held, or justice loved, by *the few*; the MILLIONS must mean *to do justly, love mercy, and walk humbly with their God.* The millions must be taught to *discuss*, not

The Failures of Popular Education.

fight; to *trust publicity*, not secrecy; and to take timely public precautions against every kind of selfish oppression.... The common schools should impart the elements of physical, mental, and moral training, and *in morals* the elements are *by far the most valuable part.*

"Concerning an educated individual, we may fairly ask, Can he see straight? can he recognize the fact? Next, can he draw a just inference from established facts? Thirdly, has he self-control? or do his passions run away with him? or untoward events daunt him? These are fair tests of his mental and moral capacity. One other test we may fairly apply to an educated individual—does he continue to grow in power and in wisdom throughout his life? His body ceases to grow at twenty-five or thirty years of age—does his soul continue to grow?"

A writer in one of England's leading magazines, of February, 1903, the *Nineteenth Century*, in an article entitled "The Disadvantages of Education," covers practically the same ground as did President Eliot in his addresses: and to the same end—the short-comings and failures of education in England, consequently the urgent demand for reform, yet with the recognition of the truth that "not only in Great Britain, but everywhere, it seems clear that it would be unreasonable to expect that the schools should reform themselves. Therefore reforms must come from outside, unless education is to remain what it is—an elaborate sham, with science in its mouth, but in reality a course of cramming, destructive to common sense."

The extracts presented in this chapter most forcibly emphasize not only the world's sore need of a better system of education, but also the world's knowledge of this need, and its longing for that which will satisfy the need. These extracts also emphasize the truth that nothing short of a system of education built upon the principles advocated in this book—true Christian education—can

The Place of the Bible in Education

ever possibly satisfy this great need of a better system of education. The defects and demands of popular education, as presented in these extracts, show that only an education that is positively Christian in the very spirit and power and morals of genuine Christianity, can ever answer the call. President Eliot, in very words, calls for such an education as will cause "the millions" of "democratic society" to "*mean to do justly*, love mercy, and walk humbly with their God." In very words his goal is "the perfecting of an intelligent individual citizenship in a *Christian* democracy."

Now it is impossible for that goal ever to be attained without a teaching, an education, that is religious and Christian. And it is impossible for *the State*, or any system of State schools, ever to attain that goal; because the State can not possibly teach religion. This is so in the nature of things; but in the United States it is doubly so, because by the fundamental principles and Constitution of the nation there is declared a total separation of the State from religion, and particularly the Christian religion. The State can no more properly or safely use the religious method in its education than the Church can use the secular method in her education. The two realms are distinct, and they can not be blended without destruction to both the Church and the State.

To the Church alone belongs the teaching of religion, the inculcation of morals, the promotion of Christianity. This is to say, therefore, that the only possibility of the better system of education ever being truly supplied, for the want of which the country is perishing, is in the Christian Church's supplying it. But lo! in the presence of this vital truth we are confronted by the deplorable fact concerning that which stands as the accepted Christian Church, that according to the words of both President Eliot and the United States Commissioner of Education, her "control over education" is a "distinctly diminishing"

The Failures of Popular Education.

quantity. This conclusion of these two high authorities among the laity is confirmed by a master of theology in the Chicago University, writing, in 1899, in the following forcible words, that every Christian heart and every observing person knows are altogether too true:—

> "There is nothing more disappointing to evangelical religion than its great schools. The fearful stress which has fallen on the...denominations during the last ten years has proceeded largely from the great schools fostered by these denominations....The very foundations of religious teaching are being undermined by teachers in our great schools, just as they have been in a large sense in the German universities. What is known as 'higher criticism' is simply working havoc with the rising minority in the three-named denominations.
>
> "There is no school on the American continent where a young man can go and learn the Bible as a whole under the direction of deeply pious and thoroughly learned teachers. There are schools where a young man fitting for the ministry can go and spend three years, and have himself stuffed with speculative philosophy under the name of theology, and with infidelity under the name of 'higher criticism.' This is a positive and a burning shame. The writer cherishes the hope that some pious man or woman of means will found a school in this country where men can be trained who will not only know the Bible from first to last, but preach it from first to last. That would be something new under the sun."

This being the attitude and condition of that which stands as the accepted Christian Church, with respect to the education which the world is longing for; and the Christian Church being the only source of hope that this need in education can ever be truly answered; it follows inevitably that there must be a reformation, a revival of vital Christianity, in these days as truly as there was before

The Place of the Bible in Education

when that failed, as that has failed, which stood as the accepted Christian Church.

President Eliot looks to education as the promising agency "to redeem and vivify the churches." That is correct; but it must be an education that comes DOWN FROM HEAVEN, not *up from the world*, to the Church. And *that education will come.* The world's longing need, its hunger and thirst, which can be supplied only through the Church from heaven, and without which it must perish, God will never leave unfilled. God still lives. His loving care for man and nations is the same today as ever of old.

Education is indeed the only agency that can redeem and vivify the Church. That education can come only from heaven and from Him who is the Head of the Church. He will send that education, and it will come. And when it comes, it will come only in and through the Word of Him who is in heaven and who is the Head of the Church. That education will be conveyed and inculcated only in "terms of creation." The Church by which this education will be given to the world will be a Church that deals and communicates only in "terms of creation." The Instructor of that Church will be the Creator Himself through the creative Word by the creative Spirit. The principles and the standard of morals of that Church will be the moral law of the Creator, as written with His own finger on the tables of stone, as demonstrated in His life on earth in the flesh, and as written by His Spirit in fleshly tables of the heart of the believer in Jesus. In all education conducted by this Church the text-book will be the Book of the Word of the Creator and Redeemer, and the study-book will be all creation and all redemption.

Thus that Church will be distinctly a universally educational Church. She will establish a system of education after this order; and will truly educate all who will receive the education. Though she will fully and truly supply that

The Failures of Popular Education.

education for which the world is longing and expressing its sore need, yet neither this Church nor the education which she gives will popular with the world. Rather she will be considered a straight-laced extremist. Nevertheless in this she will be right, absolutely and eternally right. She will be the true Church of today and for today. And the education which she will give will be the true education for today and forever.

Let all people who are longing for a better system of education, who are looking for a system that will fully supply all needs in education,—let all these open their eyes and look prayingly to see that heavenly educational Church; and God will cause them to see her. Now is her time. She must, and she will, arise and shine; and the glory of the Lord will be seen upon her. And this is the Church which Christ will present to Himself at His coming, "a glorious Church, not having spot, or wrinkle, or any such thing; but...holy and without blemish."

Studies in Christian Education

A course of lectures given by author Dr. E. A. Sutherland as a model for a system of Christian Education.

Christian Patriotism

A. T. Jones explores what is at stake regarding the origin of the unification of the church and the state.

Other Titles from TEACH Services, Inc.

National Sunday Law

A report of A. T. Jones' argument made concerning the National Sunday Bill that was introduced by Senator Blair in the 50th Congress.

Empires of the Bible

A. T. Jones tells the story of the ancient civilizations of the Old Testament from the Tower of Babel to the Babylonian captivity.

We invite you to view the complete
selection of titles we publish at:

www.TEACHServices.com

or write or email us your praises,
reactions, or thoughts about this
or any other book we publish at:

TEACH Services, Inc.
P U B L I S H I N G
www.TEACHServices.com
P.O. Box 954
Ringgold, GA 30736

info@TEACHServices.com

TEACH Services, Inc. titles may be purchased in bulk for educational, business, fund-raising, or sales promotional use. For information, please e-mail

BulkSales@TEACHServices.com.

Finally, if you are interested in seeing
your own book in print, please contact us at

publishing@teachservices.com.

We would be happy to review your manuscript for free.

www.ingramcontent.com/pod-product-compliance
Lightning Source LLC
Chambersburg PA
CBHW070549160426
43199CB00014B/2437